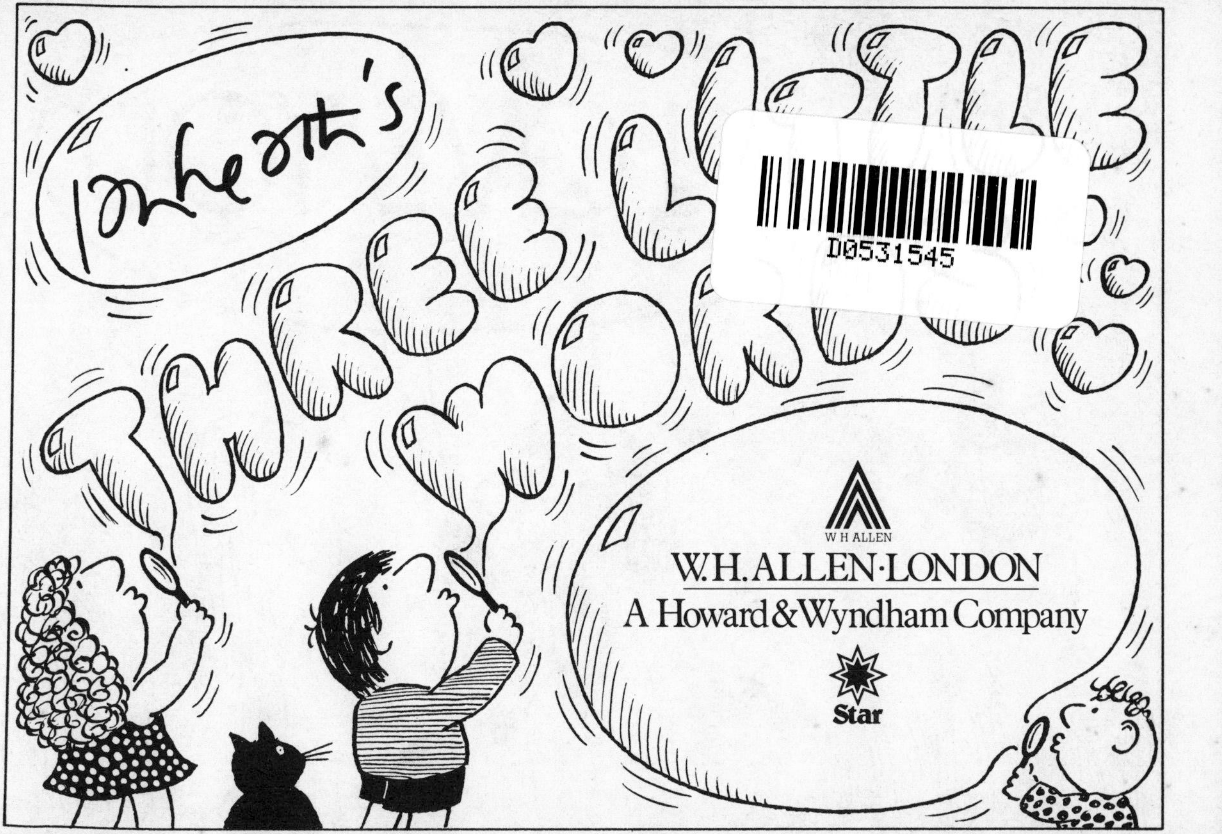

Ian Heath's
THREE
W H ALLEN
W.H. ALLEN·LONDON
A Howard & Wyndham Company
Star

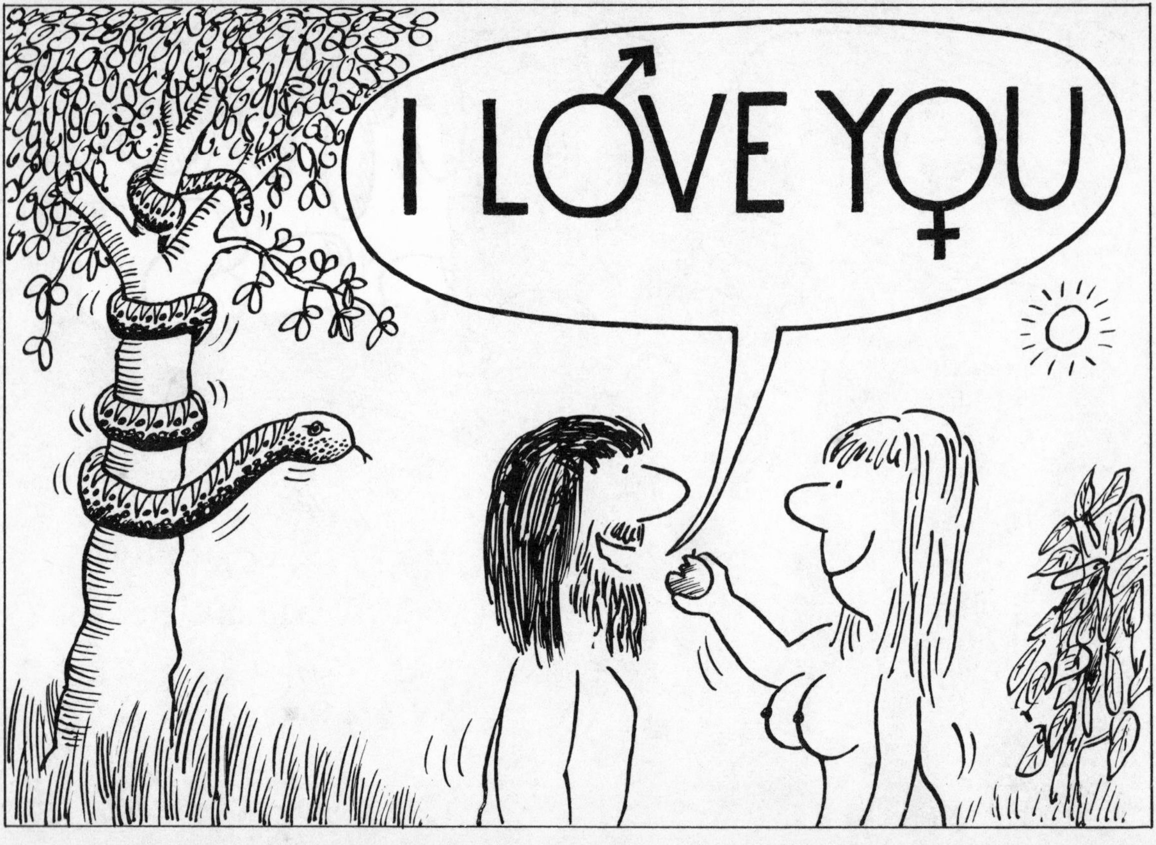
I LOVE YOU

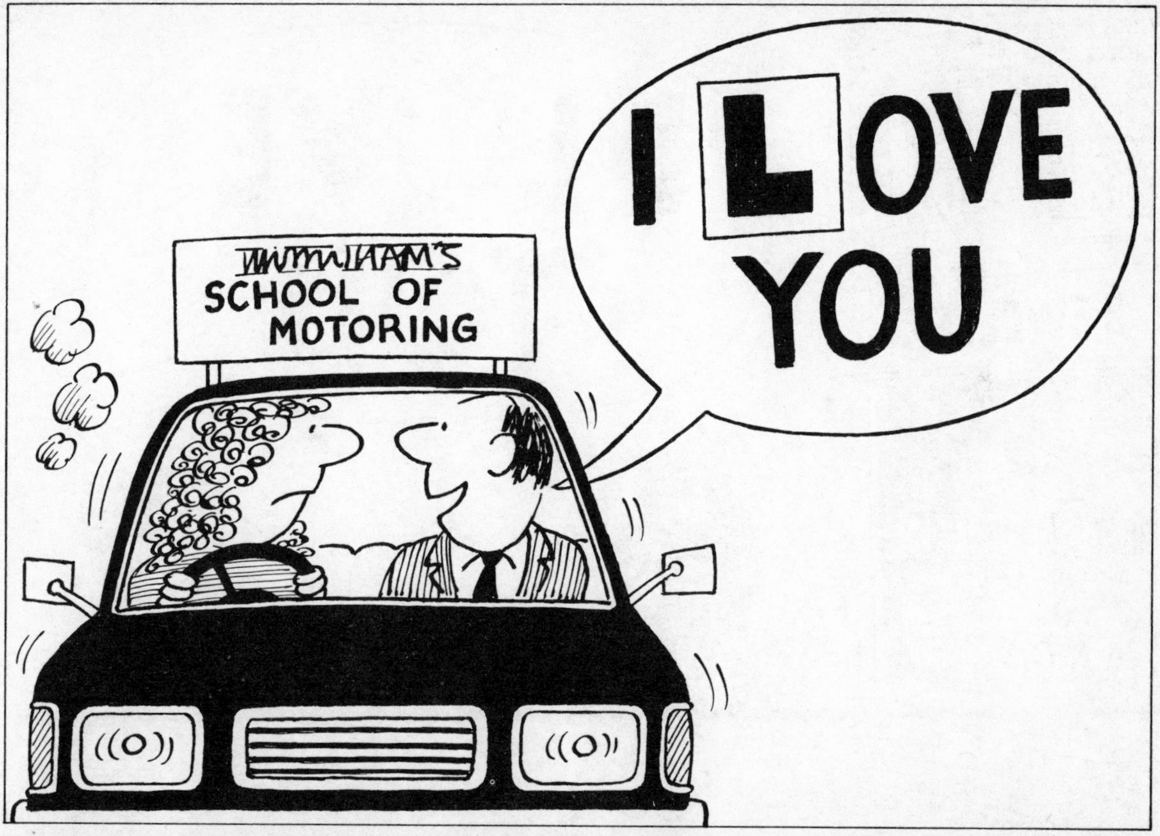
SCHOOL OF
MOTORING
I LOVE
YOU

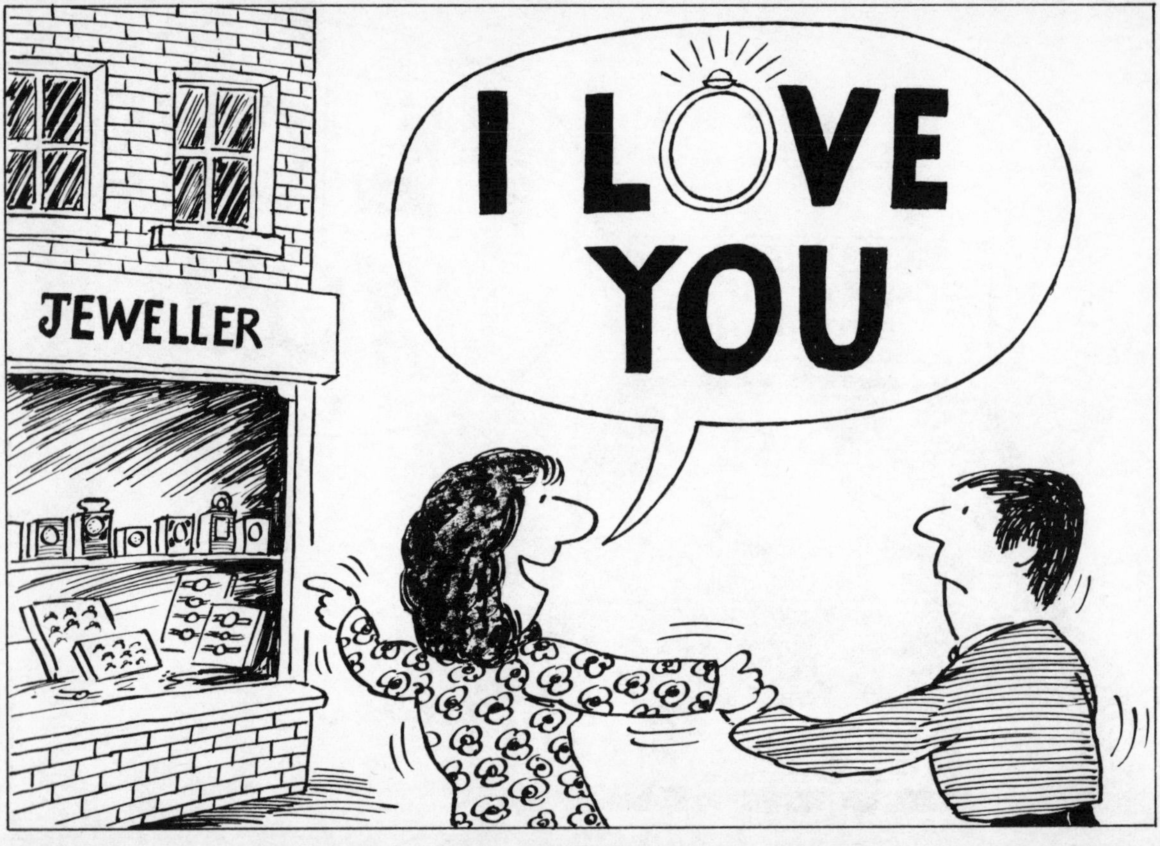
JEWELLER
I LOVE YOU

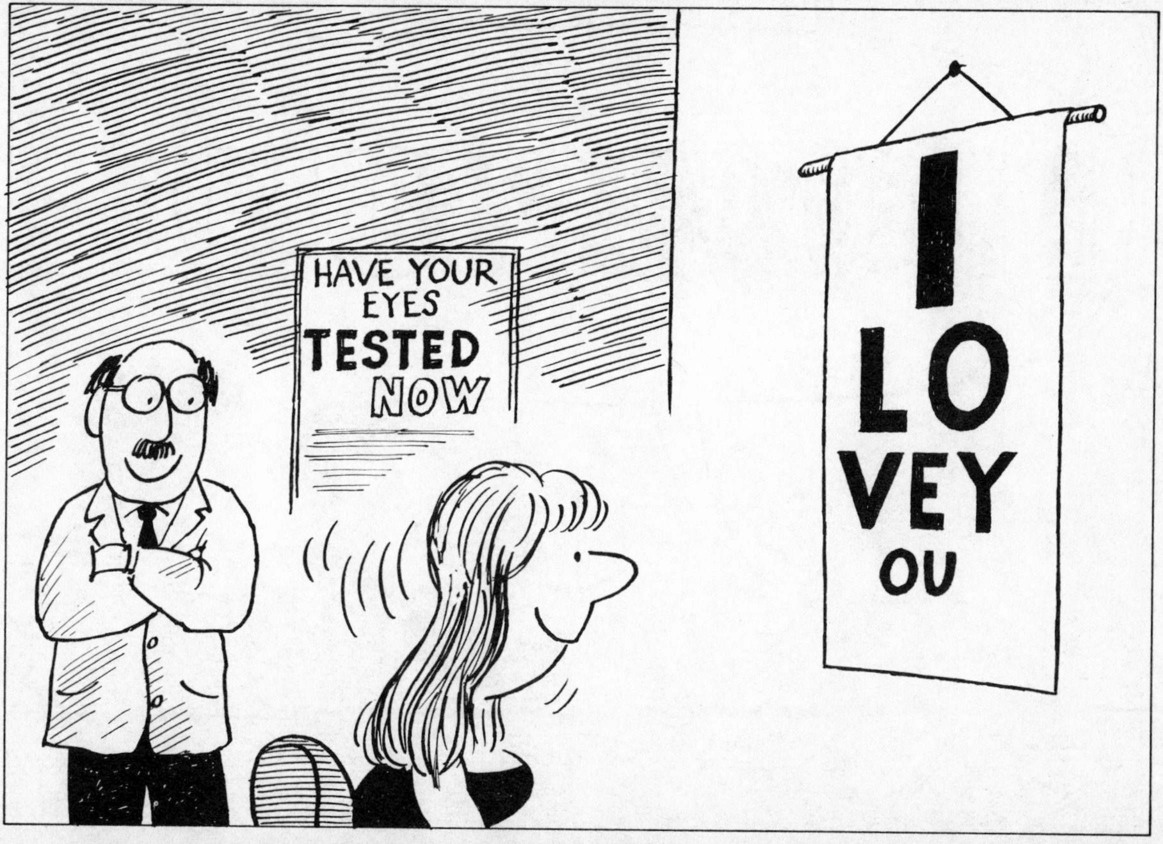
HAVE YOUR EYES TESTED NOW
I
LO
VEY
OU

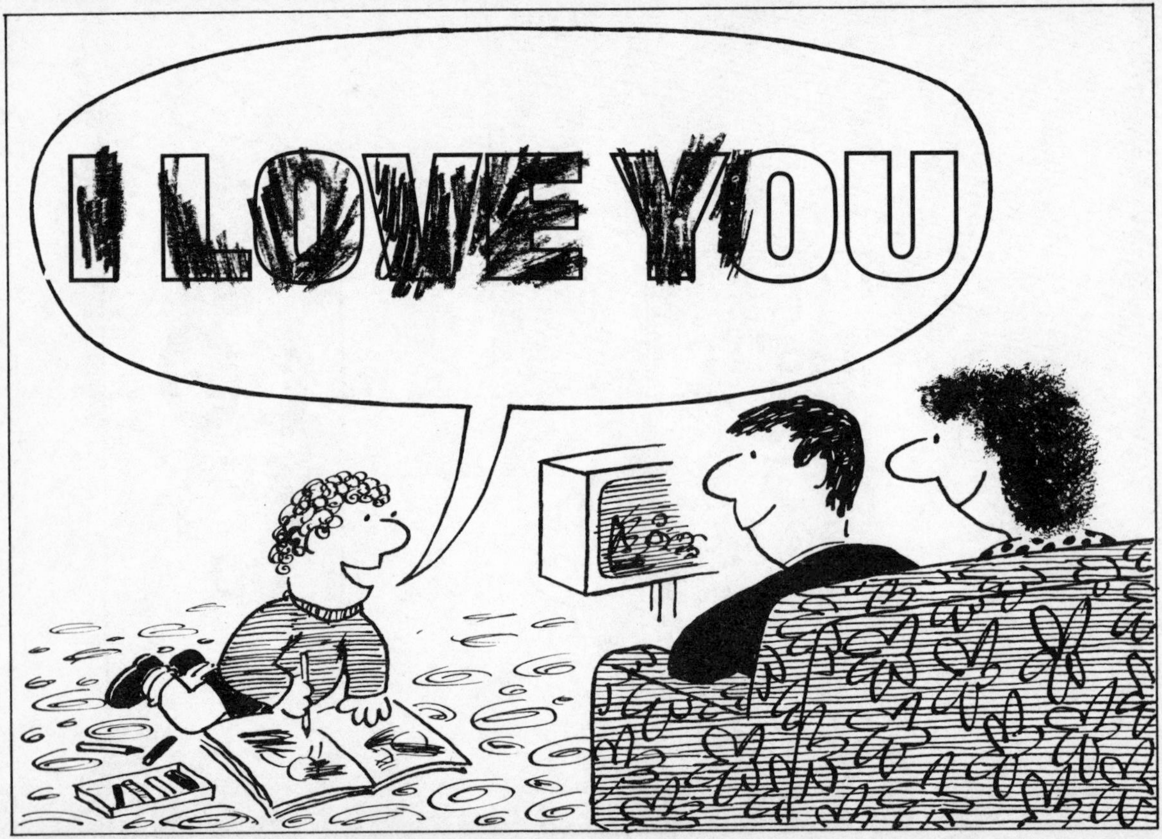
I LOVE YOU

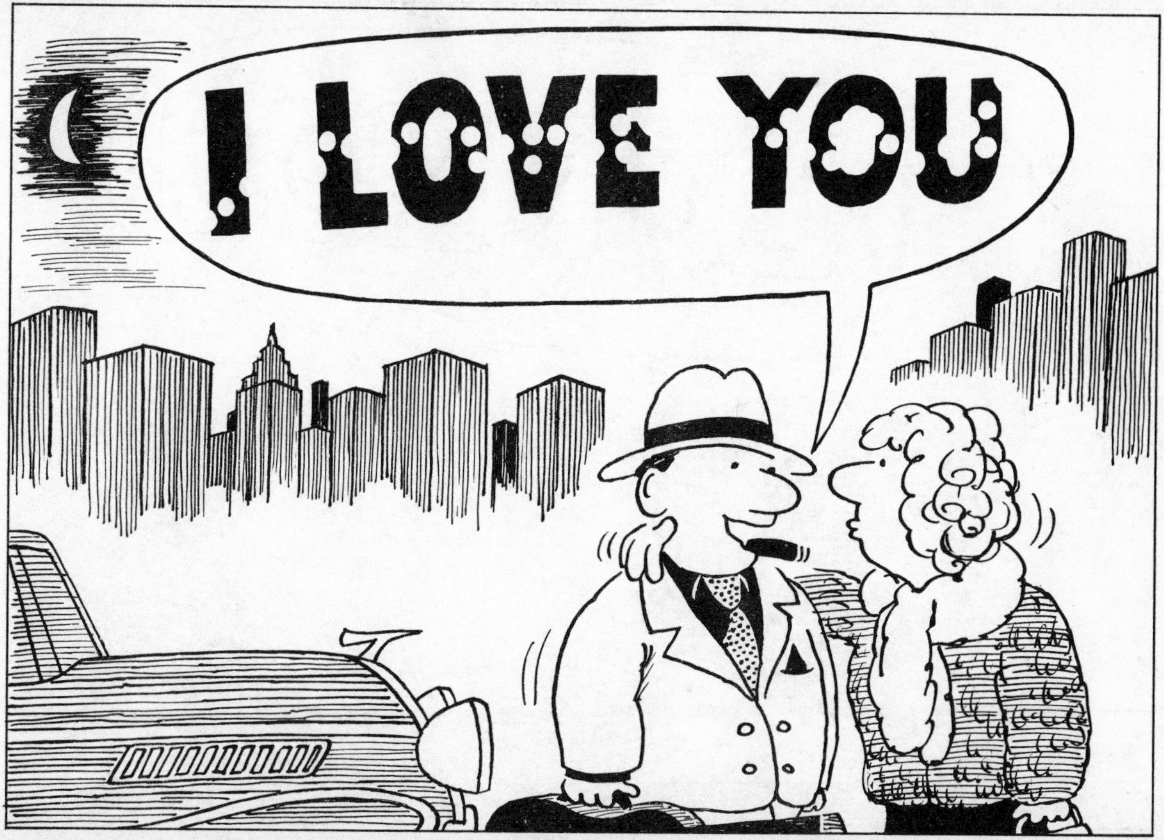
I LOVE YOU

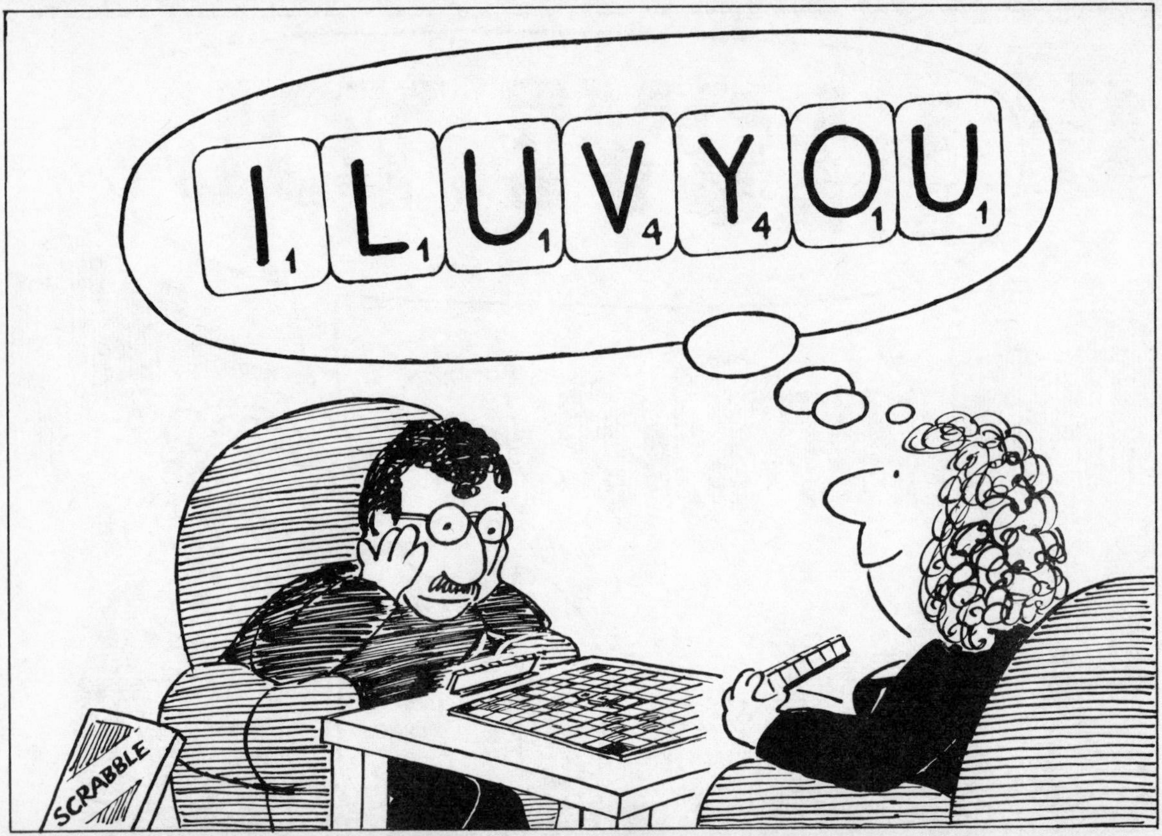
I1 L1 U1 V4 Y4 O1 U1
SCRABBLE

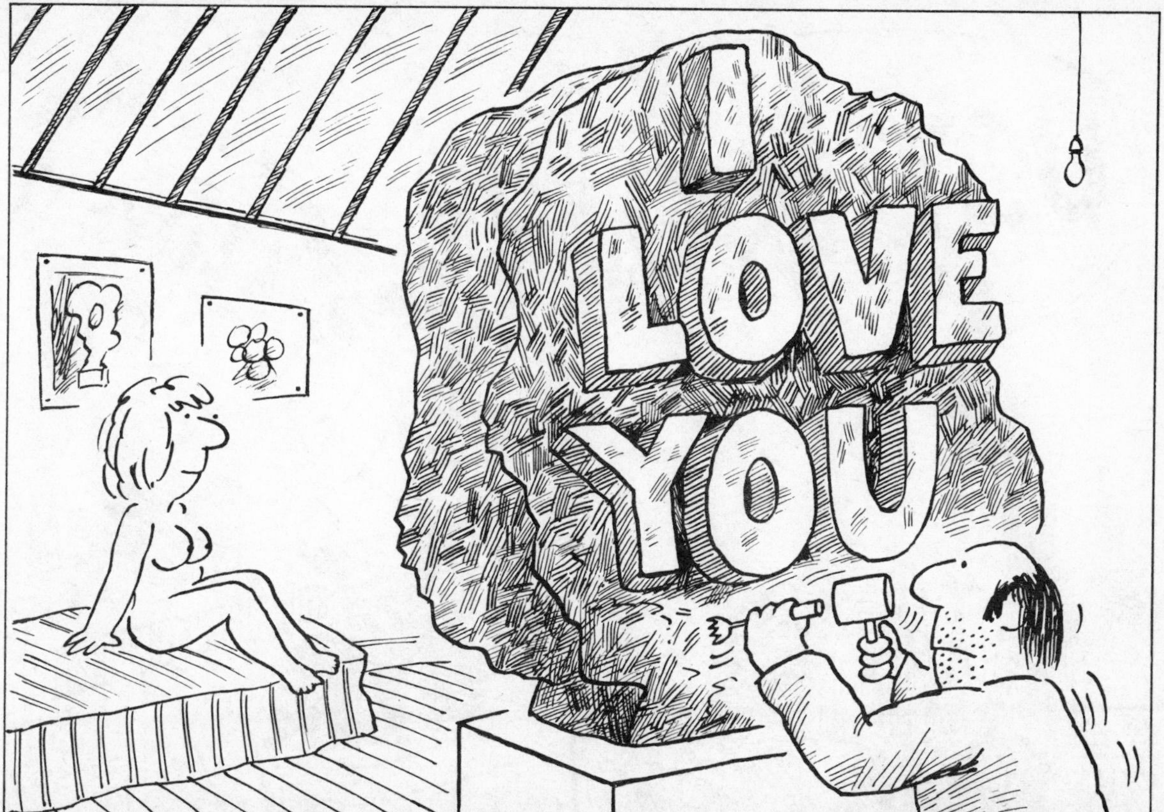
I LOVE YOU

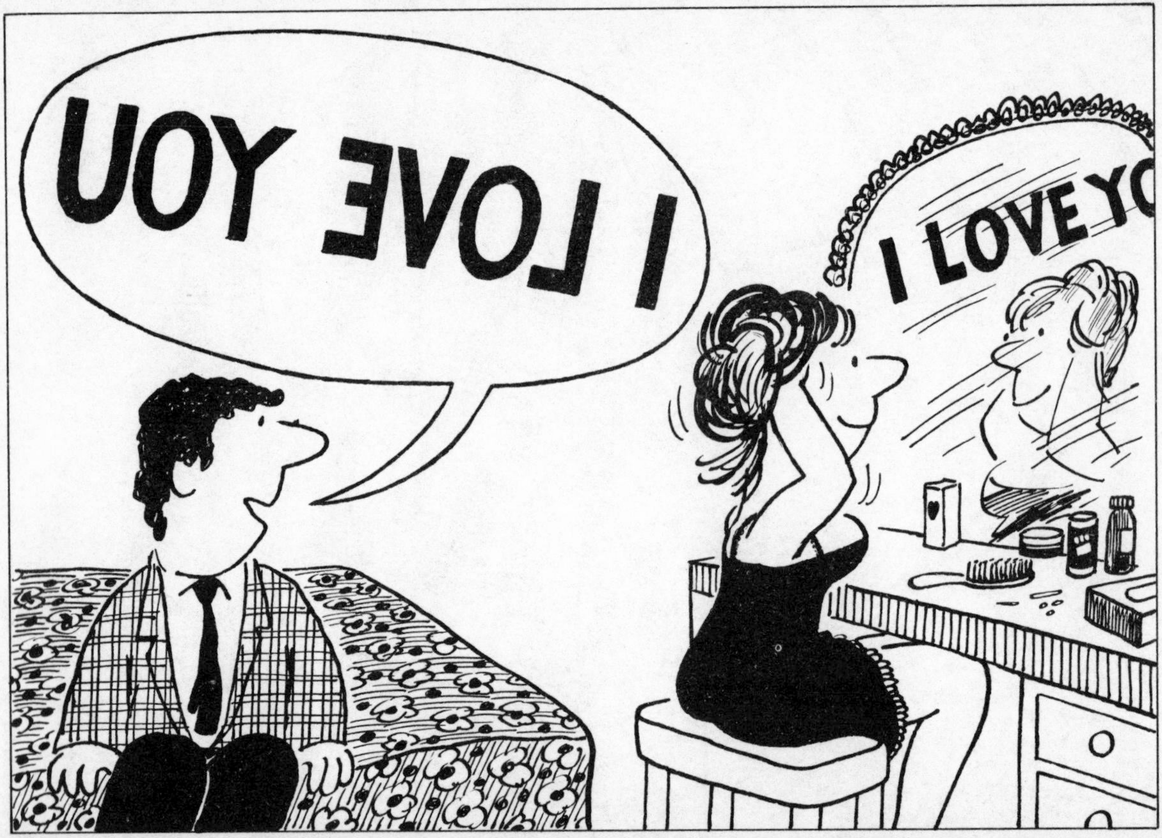

I LOVE YOU
I LOVE YO

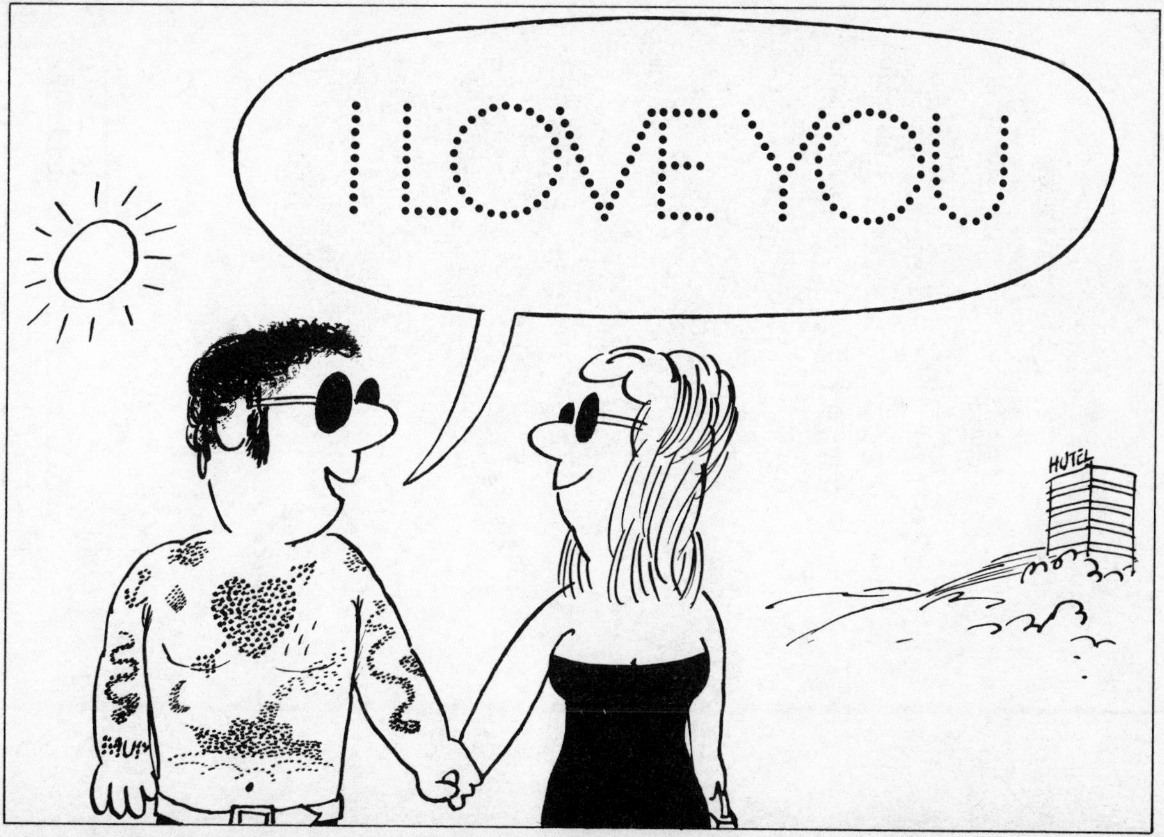
I LOVE YOU
HOTEL

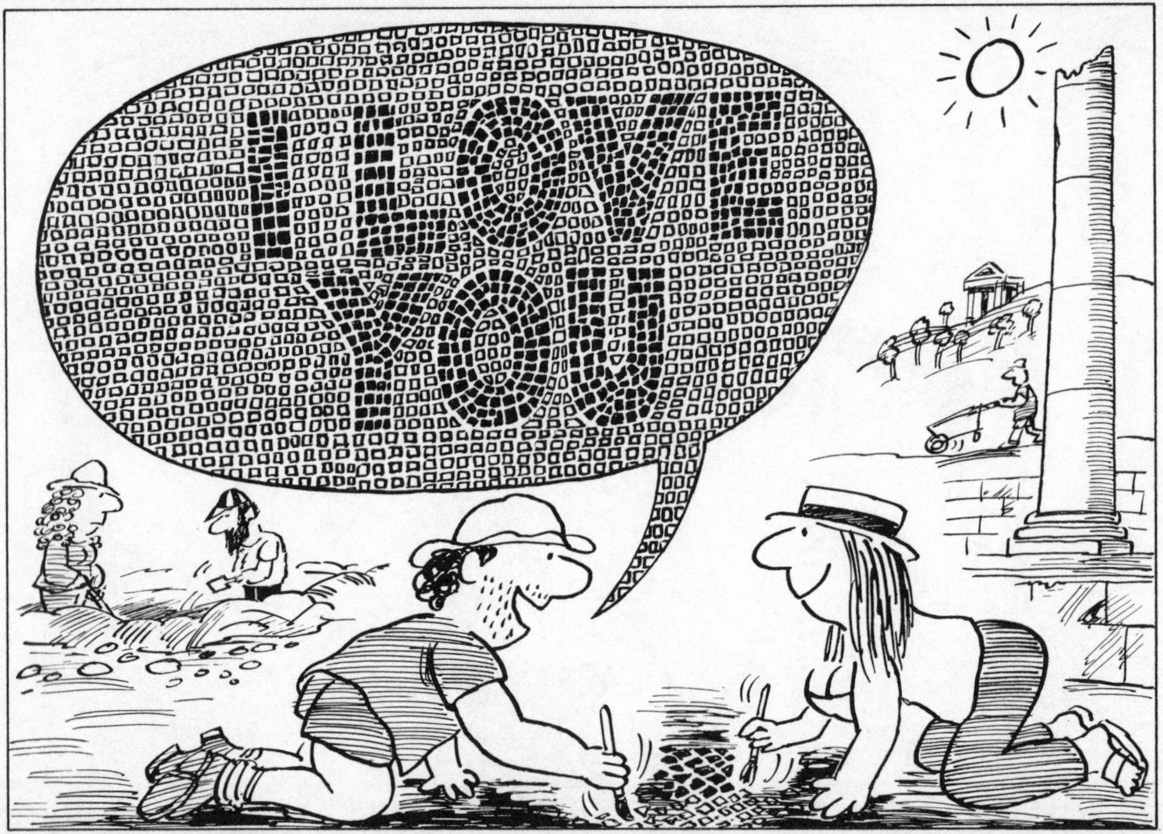
I LOVE YOU

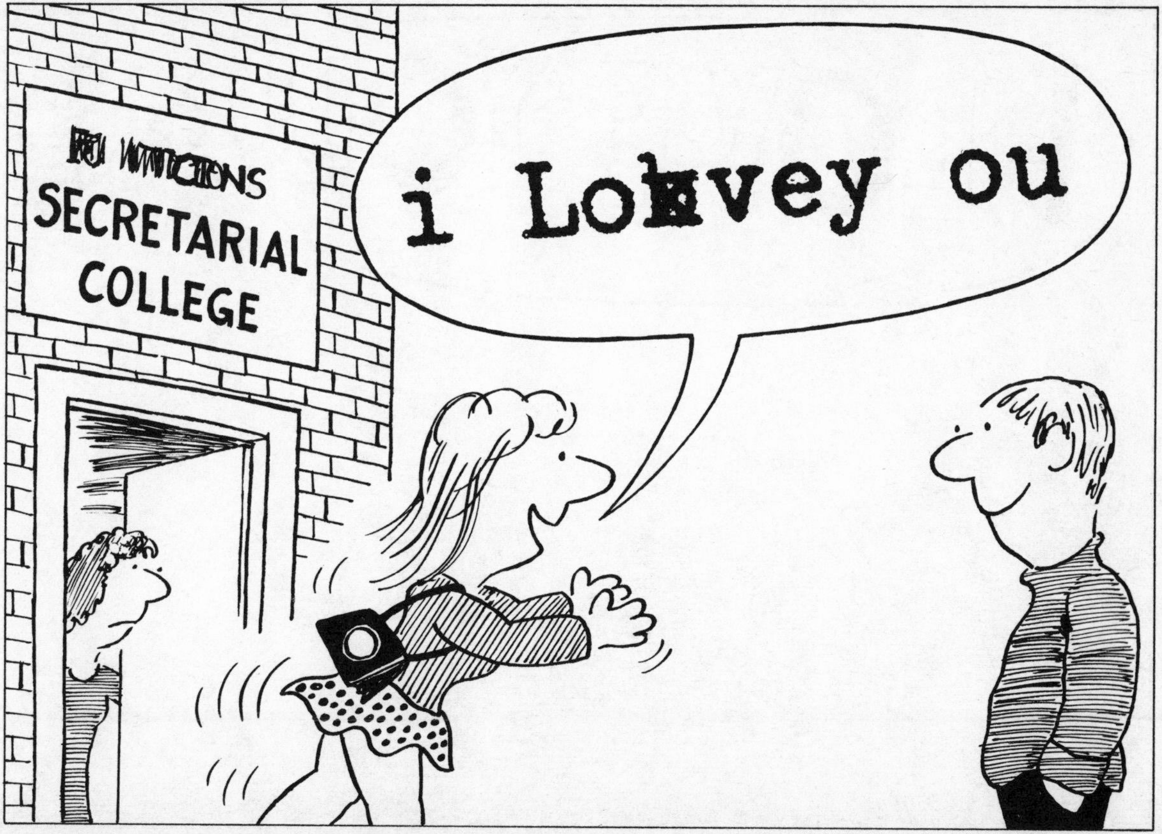
SECRETARIAL
COLLEGE
i Lohvey ou

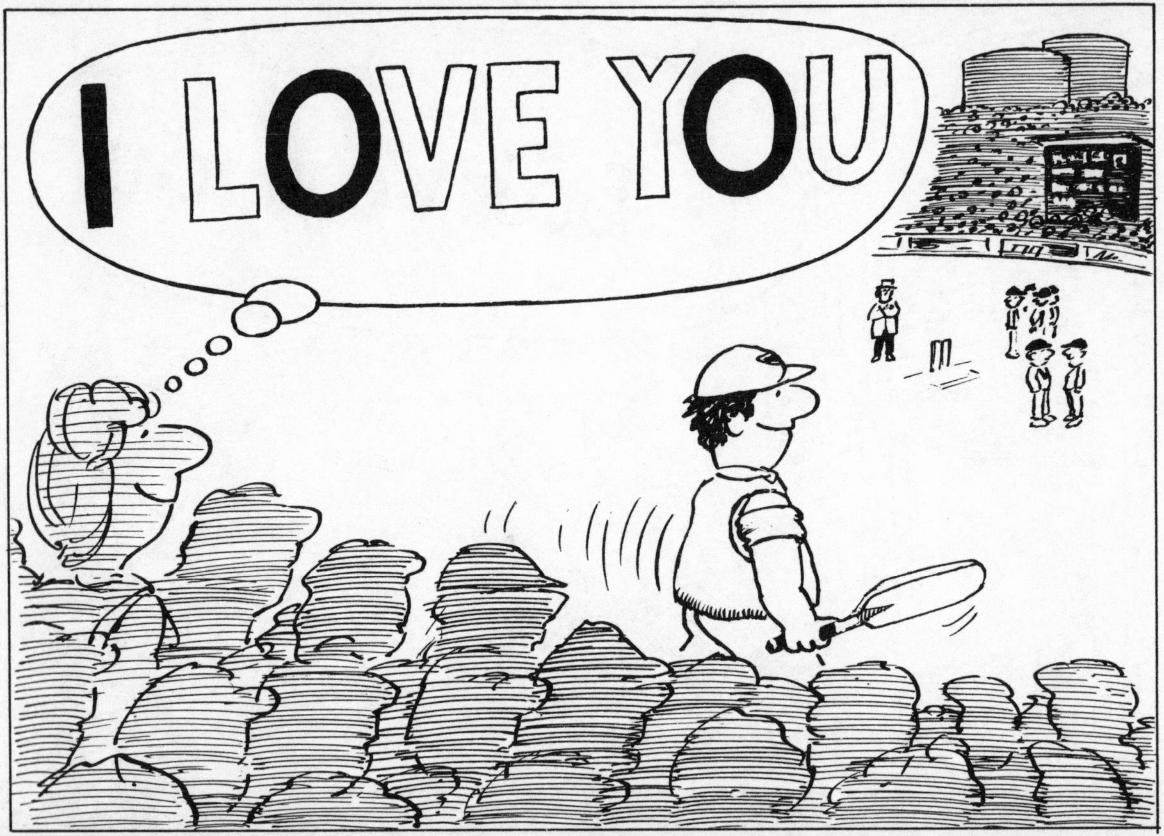
I LOVE YOU

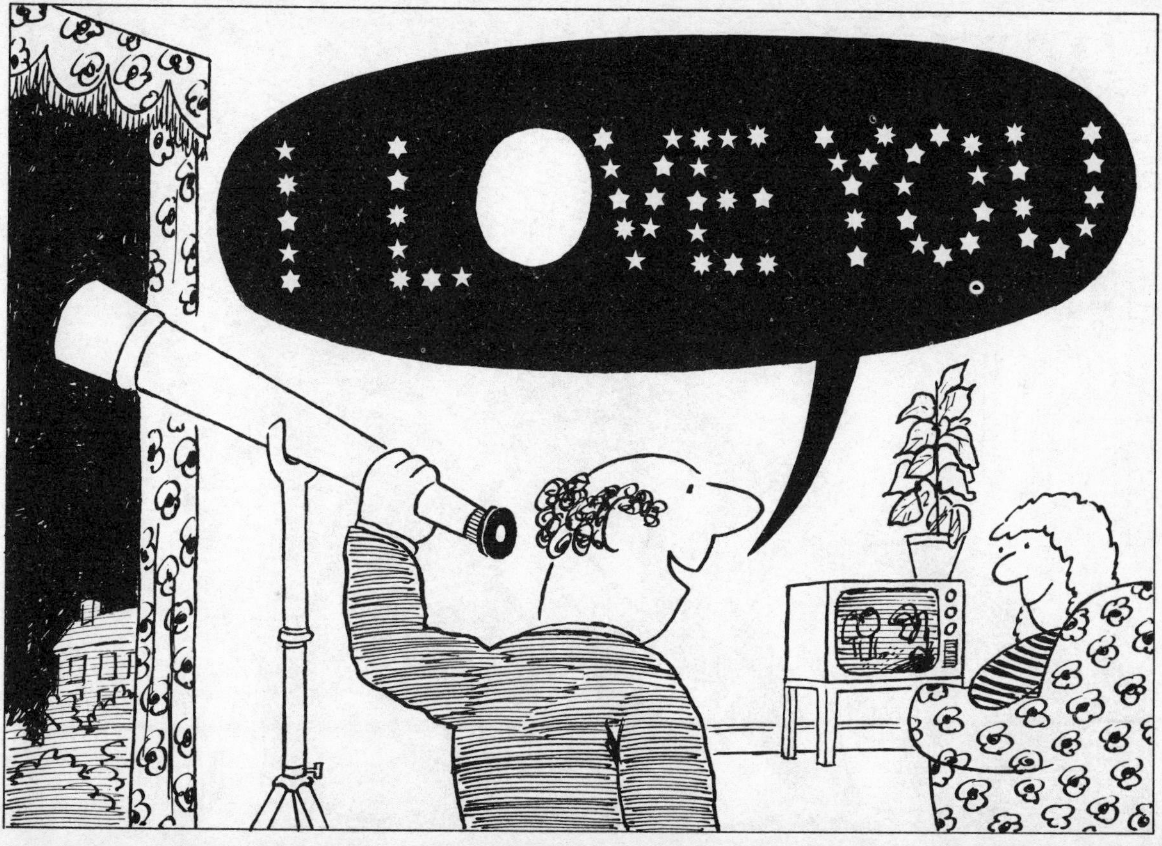

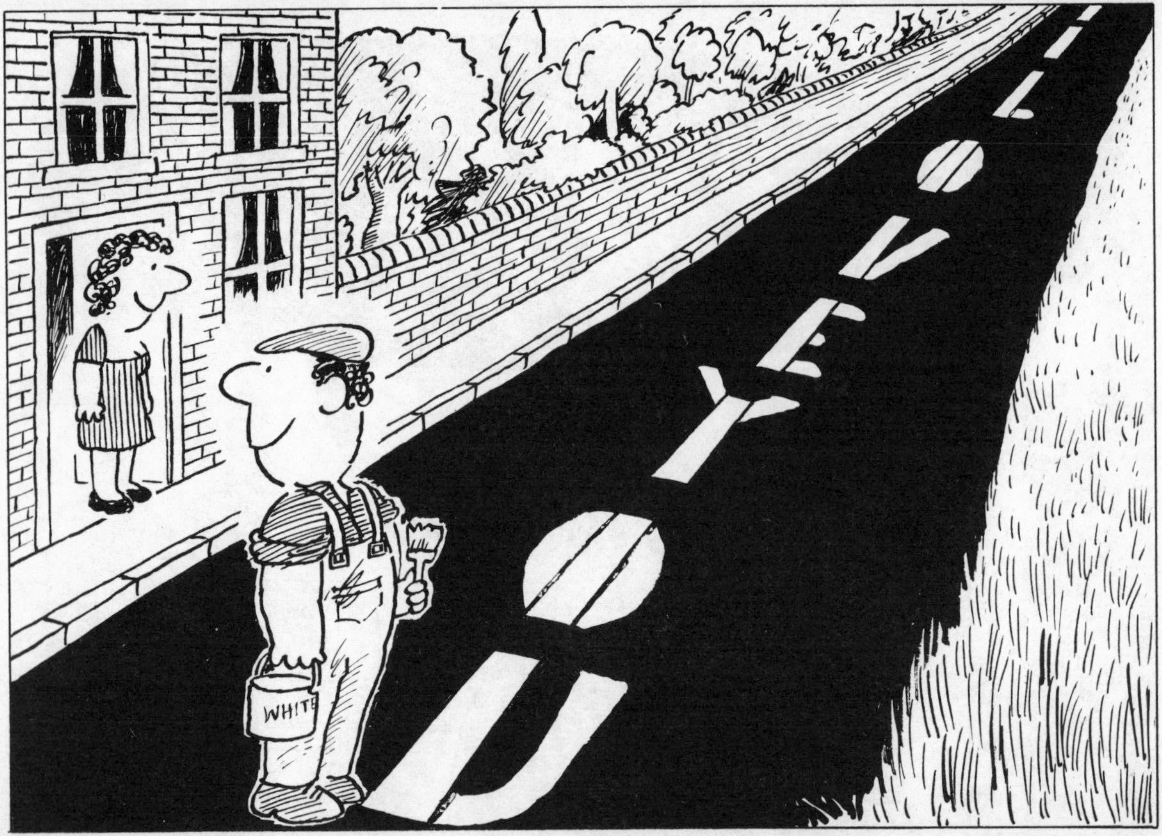
LOVE YOU
WHITE

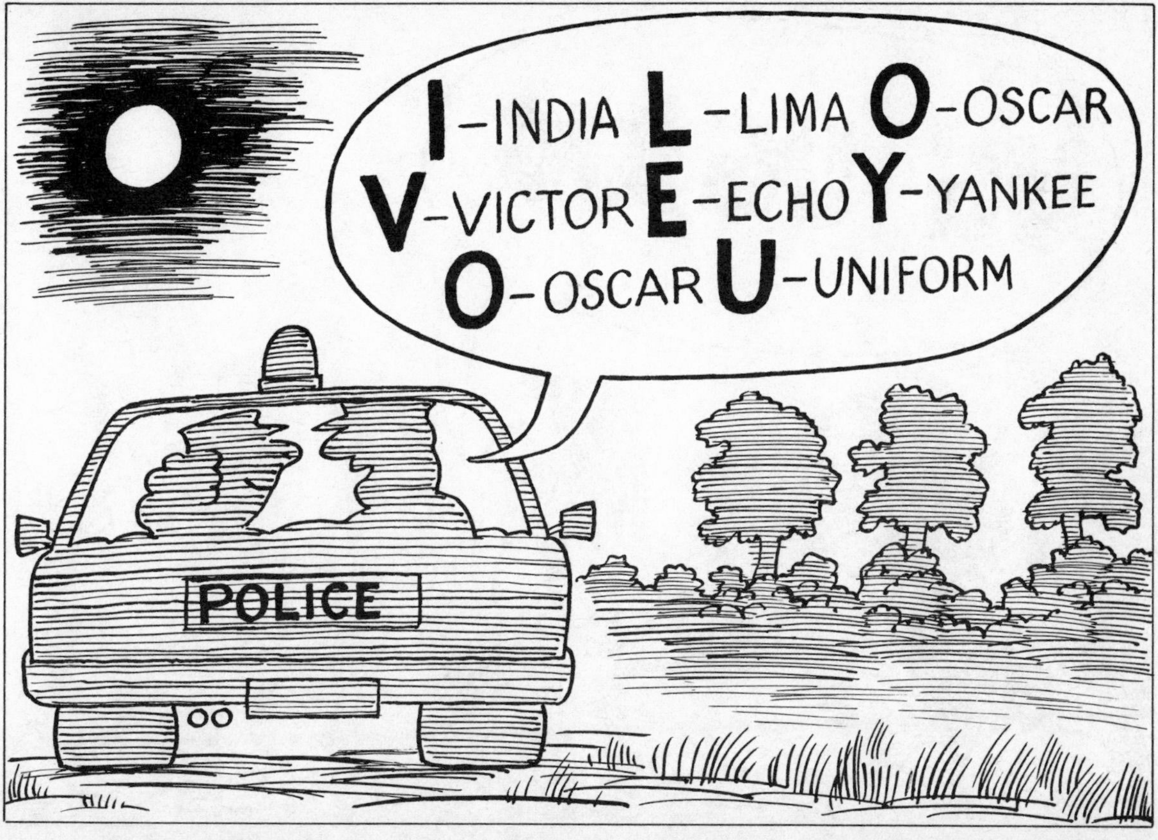
I-INDIA L-LIMA O-OSCAR
V-VICTOR E-ECHO Y-YANKEE
O-OSCAR U-UNIFORM
POLICE

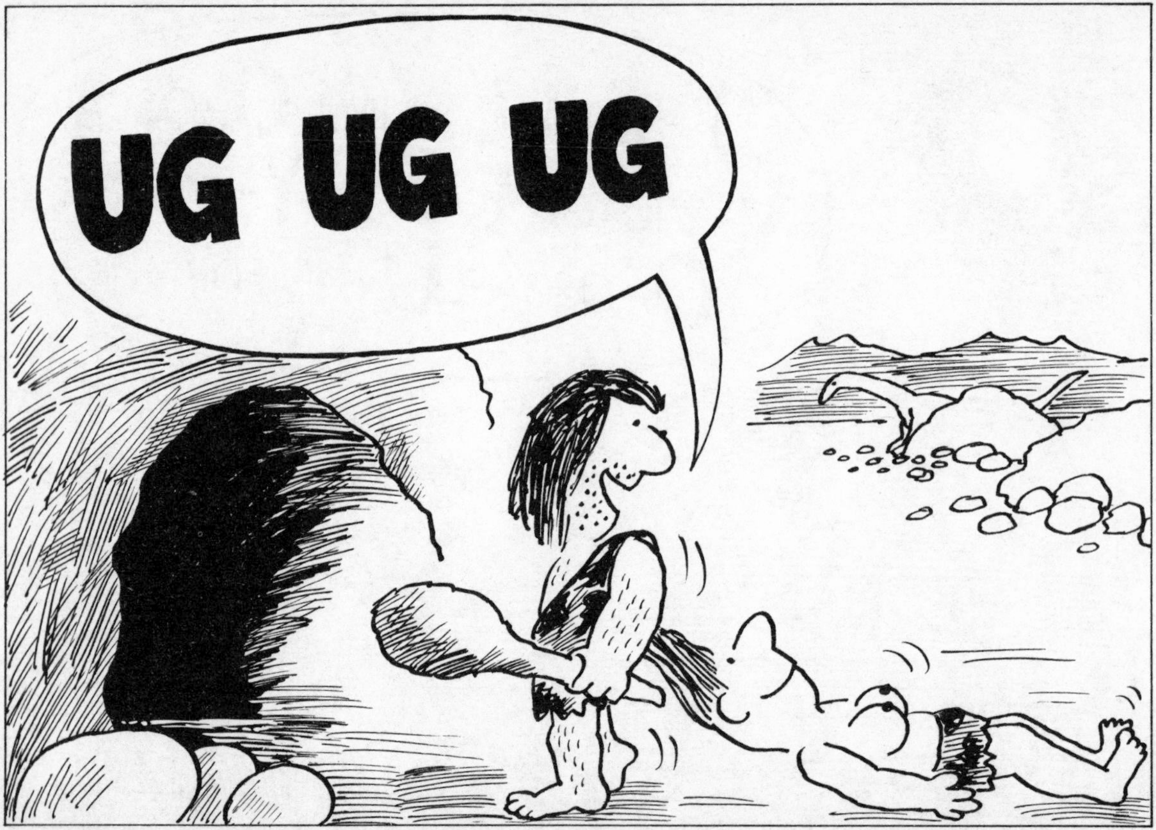
UG UG UG

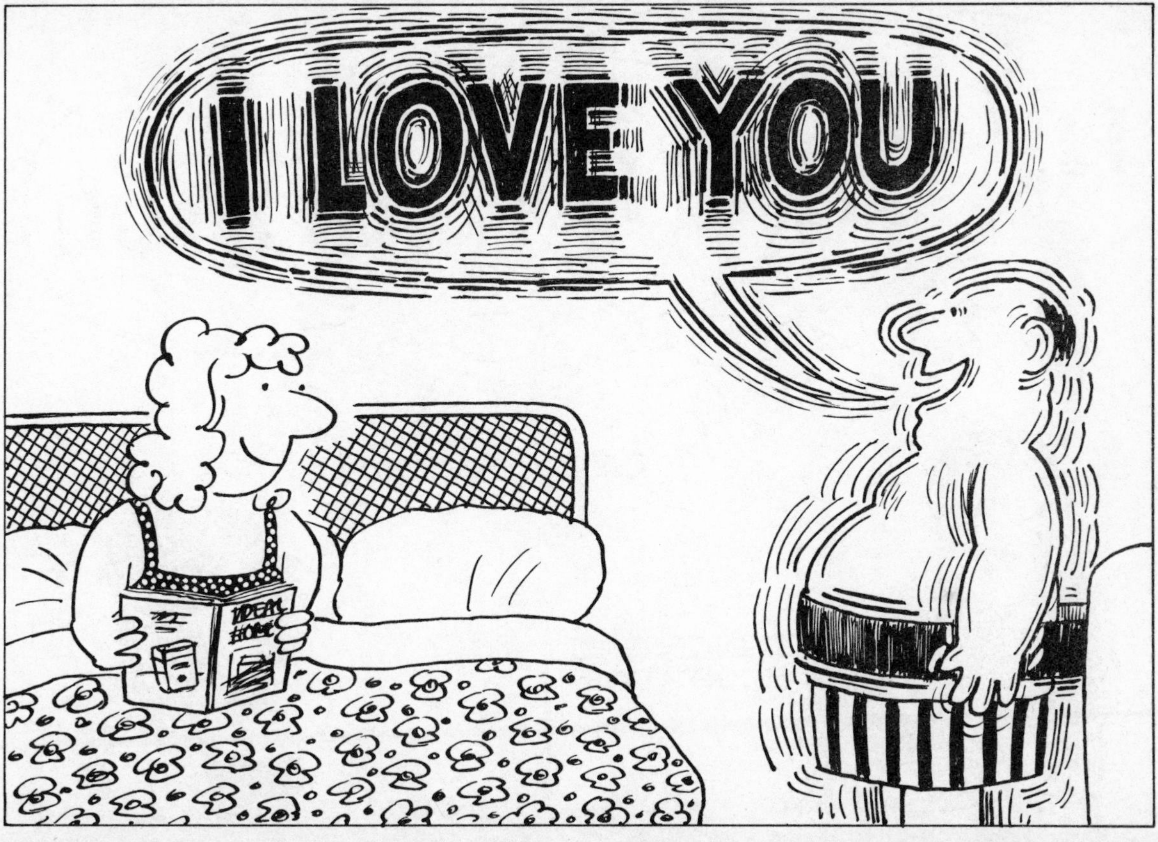
I LOVE YOU
IDEAL HOME

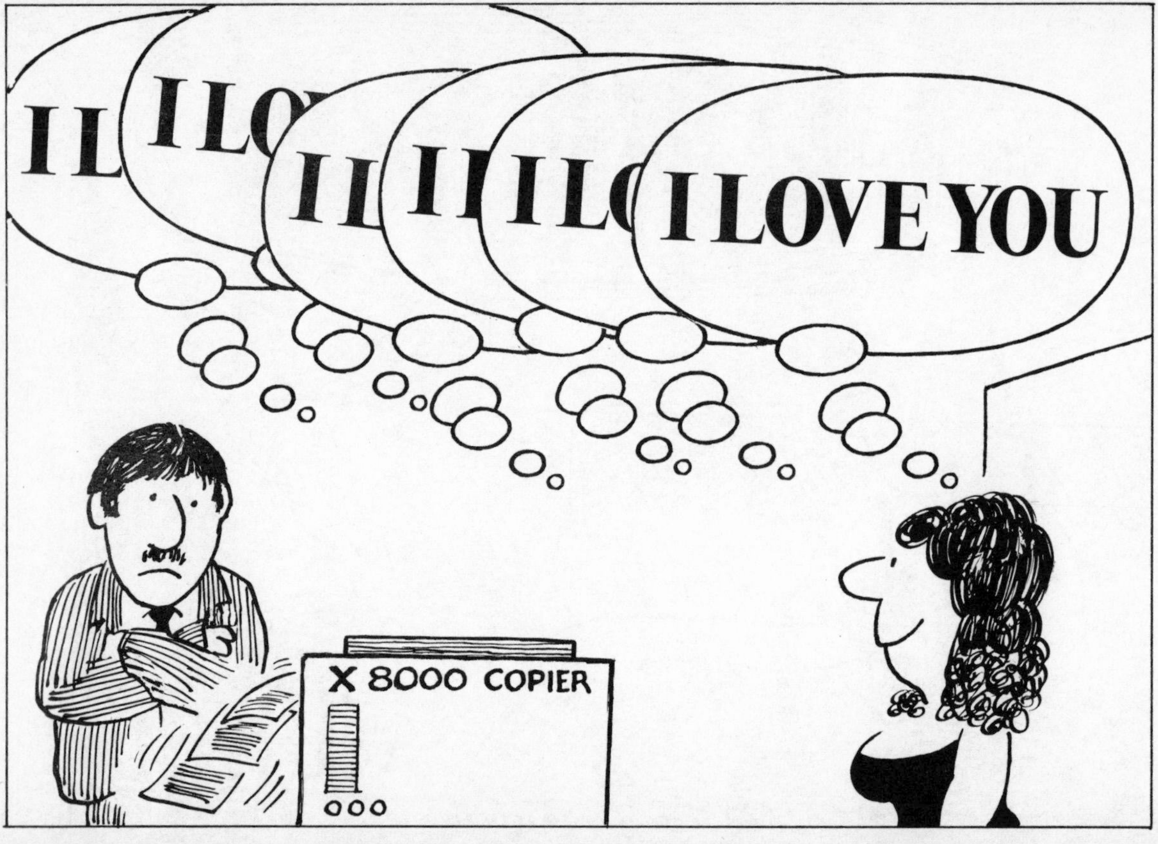
I LOVE YOU
X 8000 COPIER

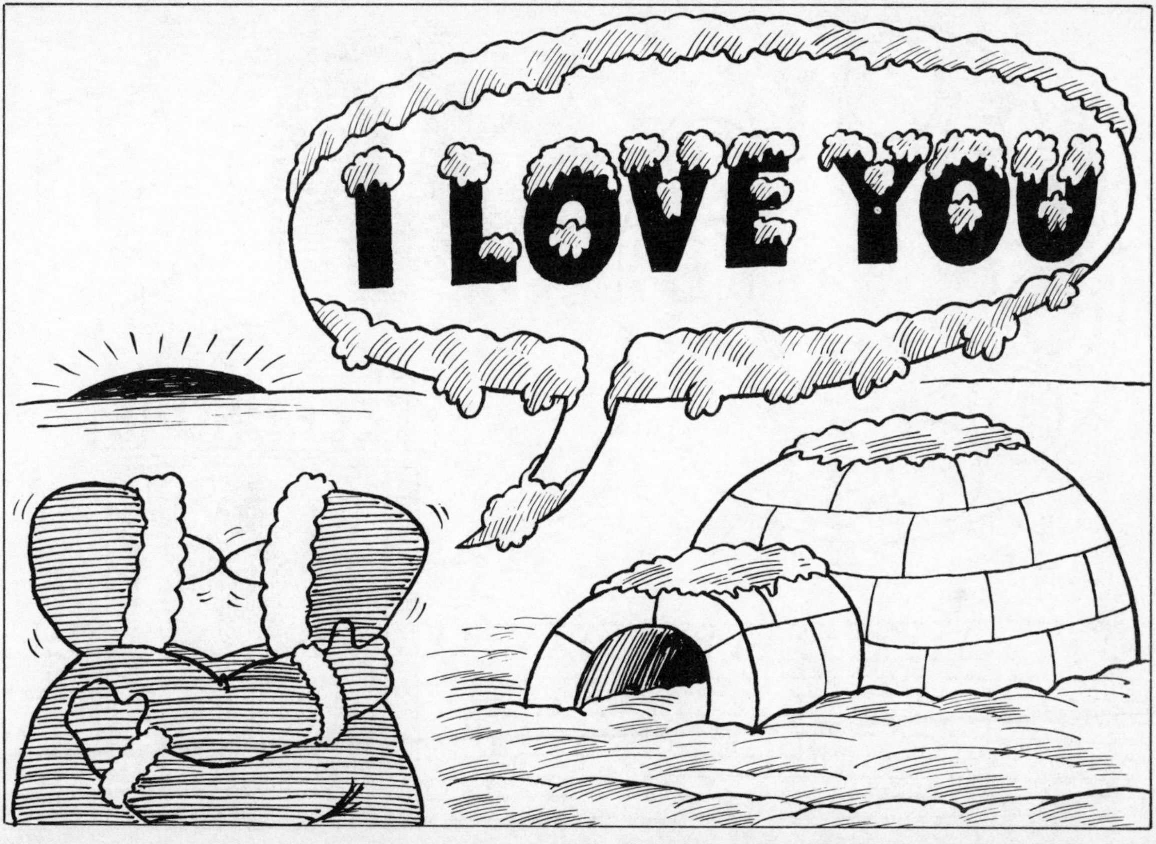
I LOVE YOU

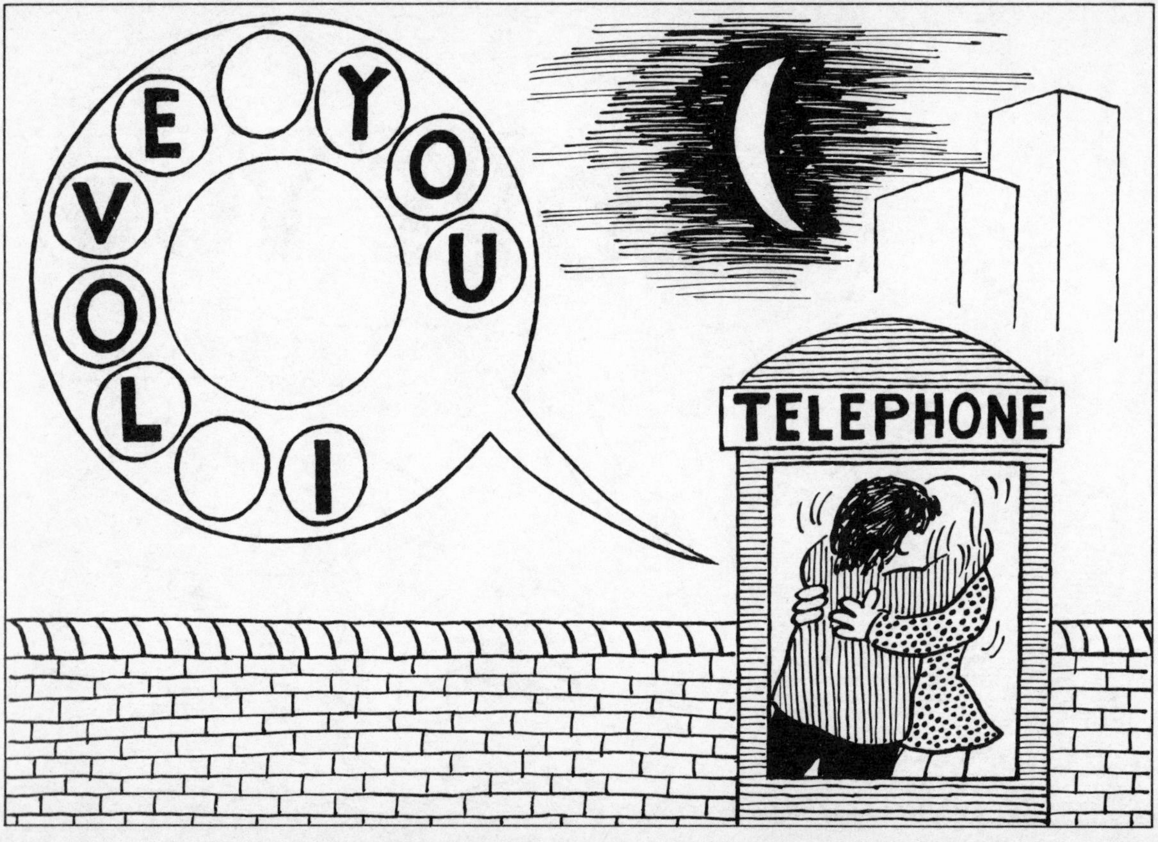
I LOVE YOU
TELEPHONE

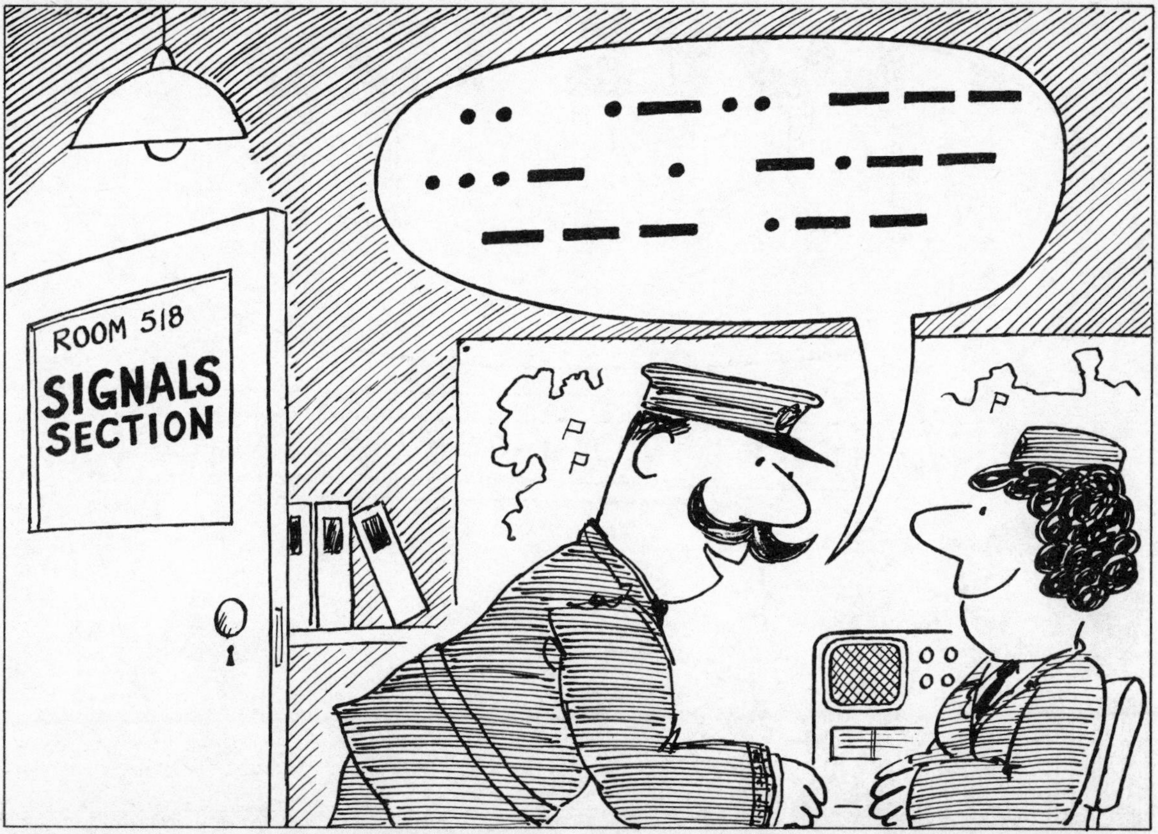
.. .-.. ---
...- . -.--
--- .--
ROOM 518
SIGNALS SECTION

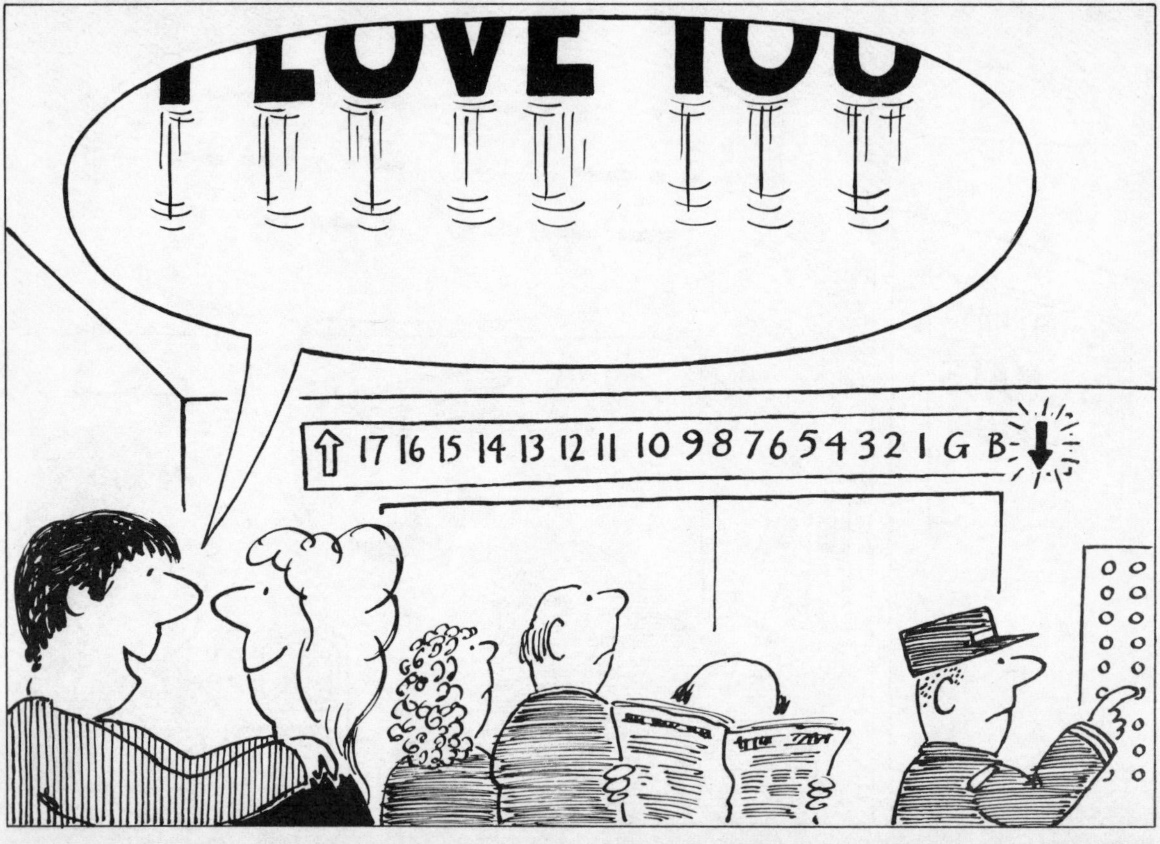
I LOVE YOU
17 16 15 14 13 12 11 10 9 8 7 6 5 4 3 2 1 G B

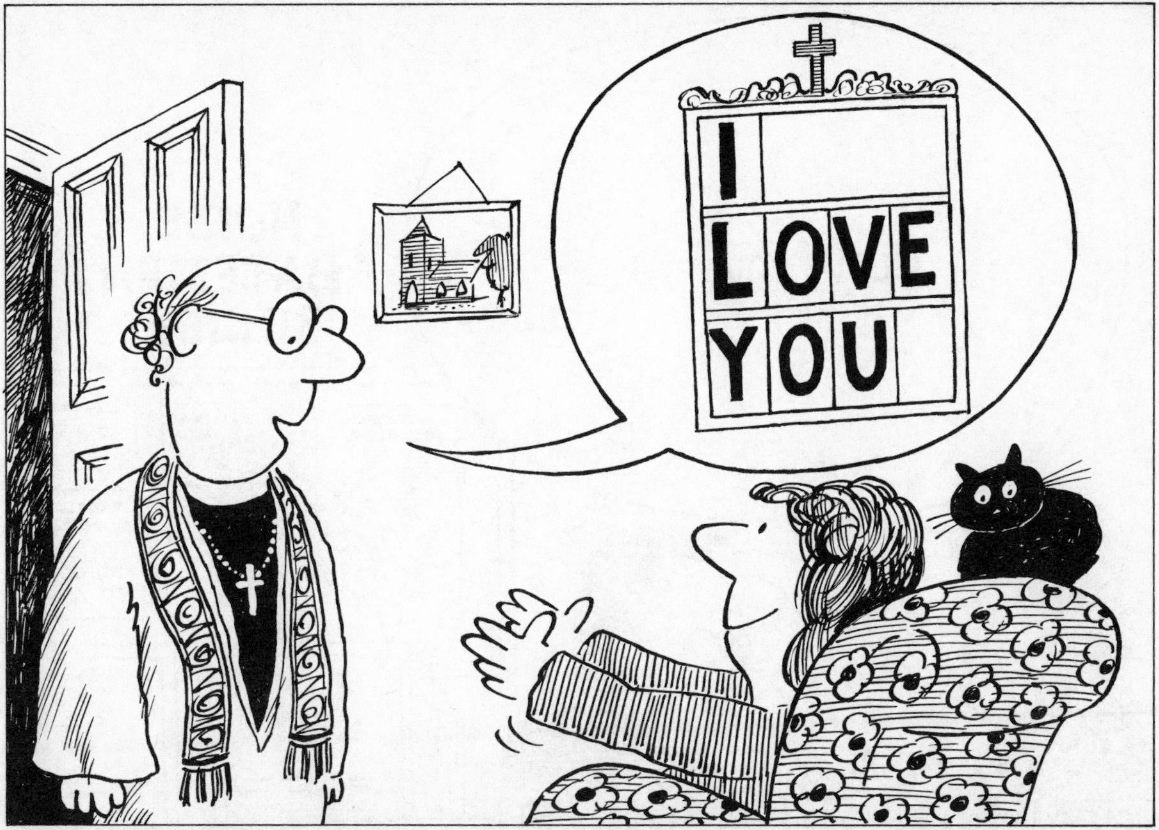
I LOVE YOU

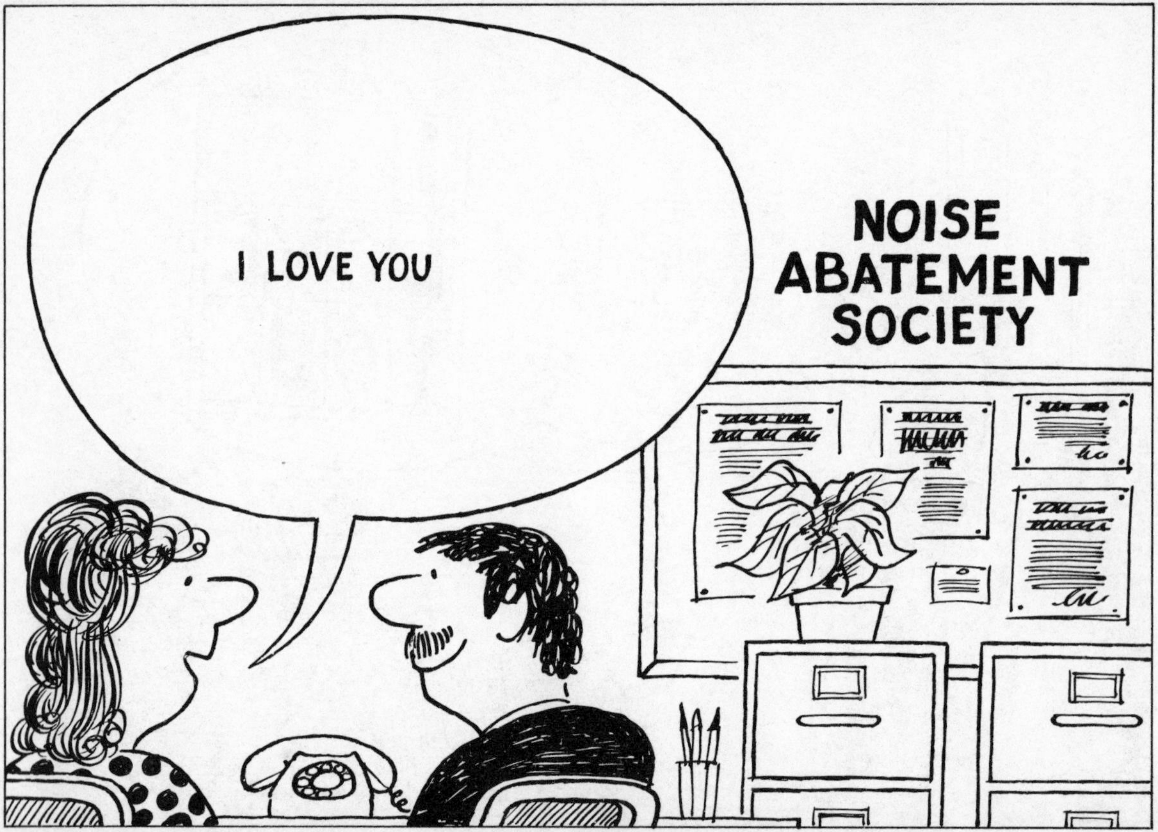
I LOVE YOU
NOISE ABATEMENT SOCIETY

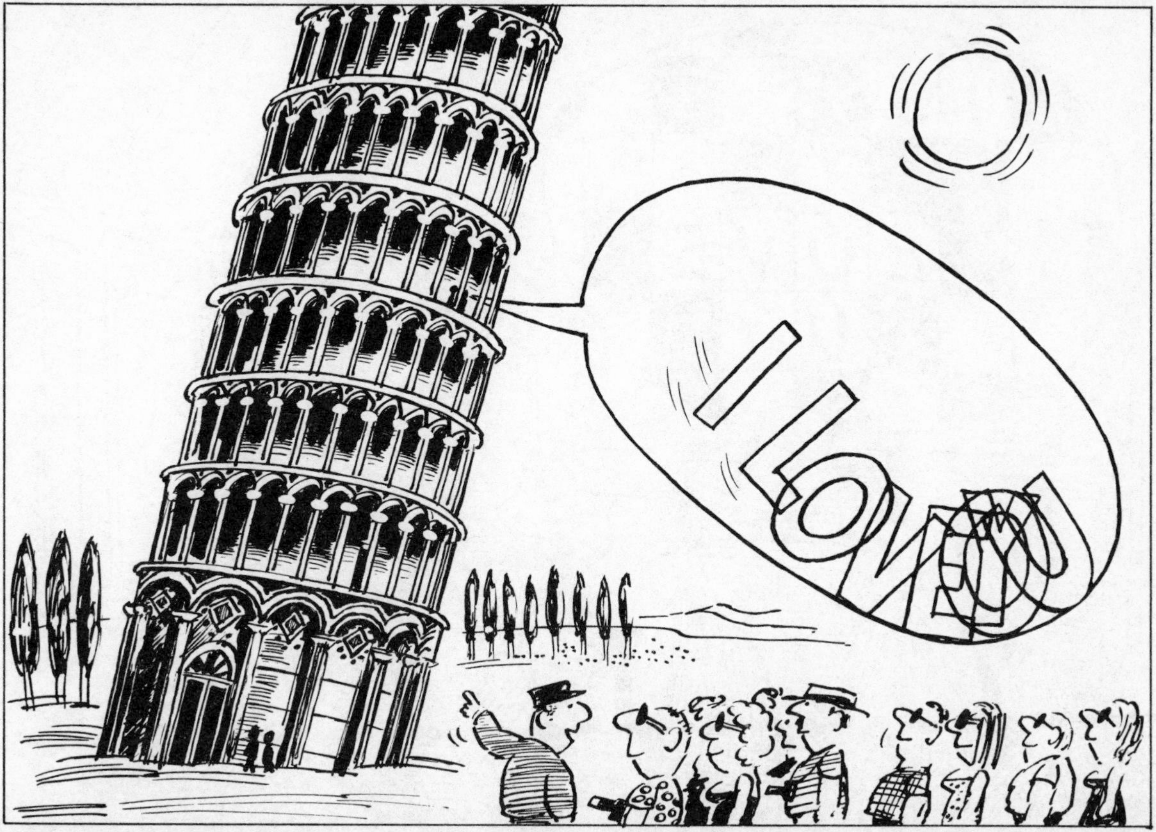
I LOVE YOU

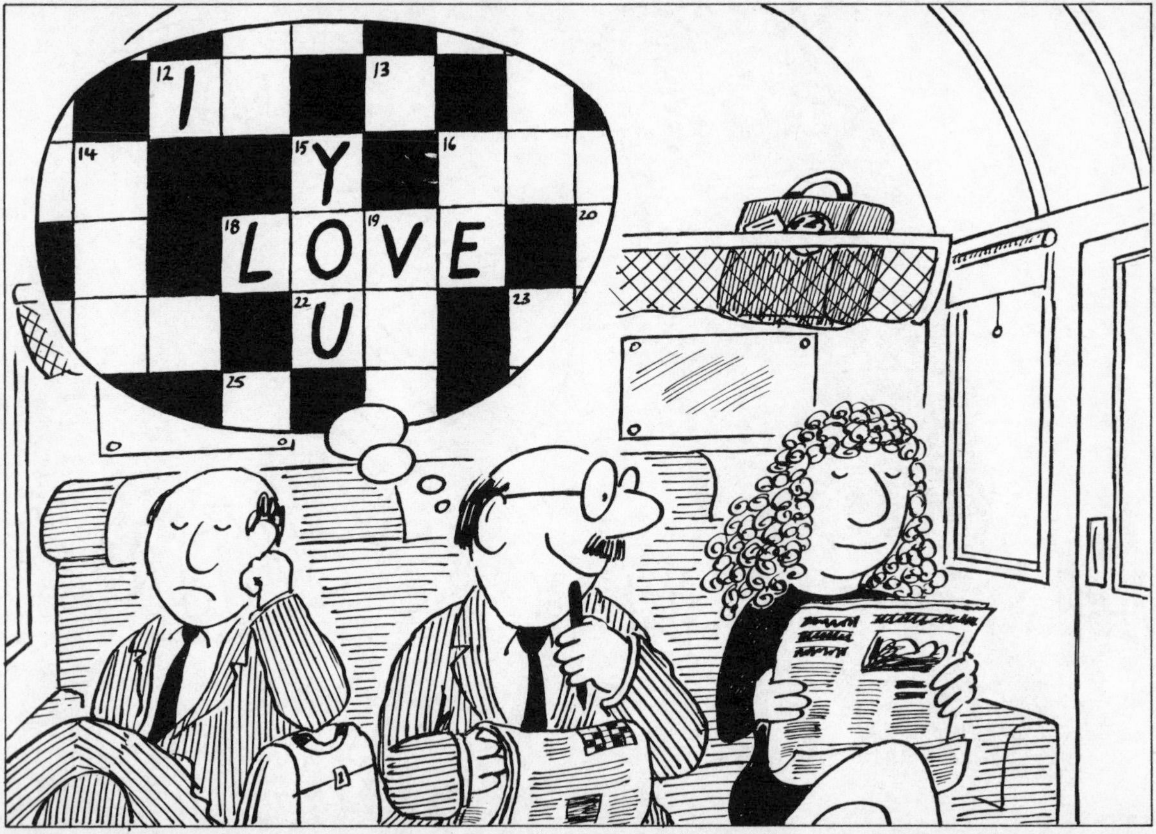
I
Y
LOVE
U

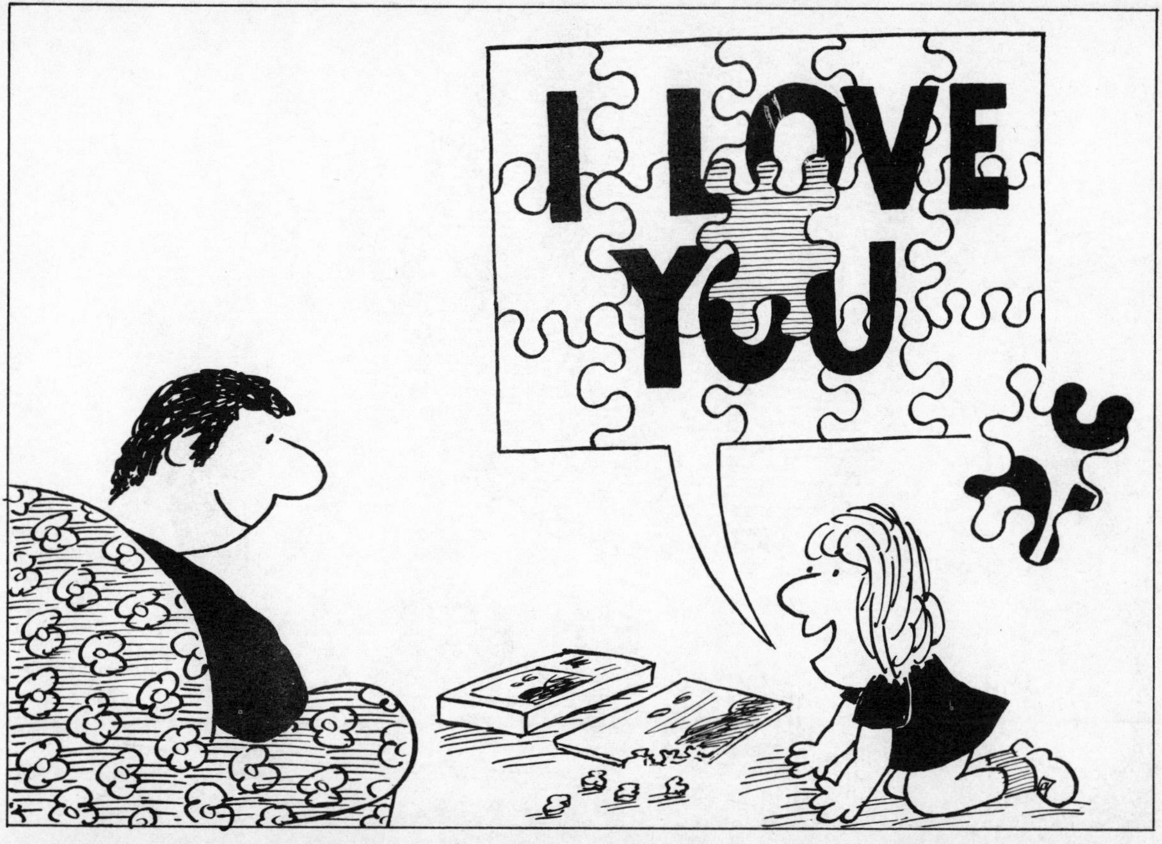
I LOVE YOU

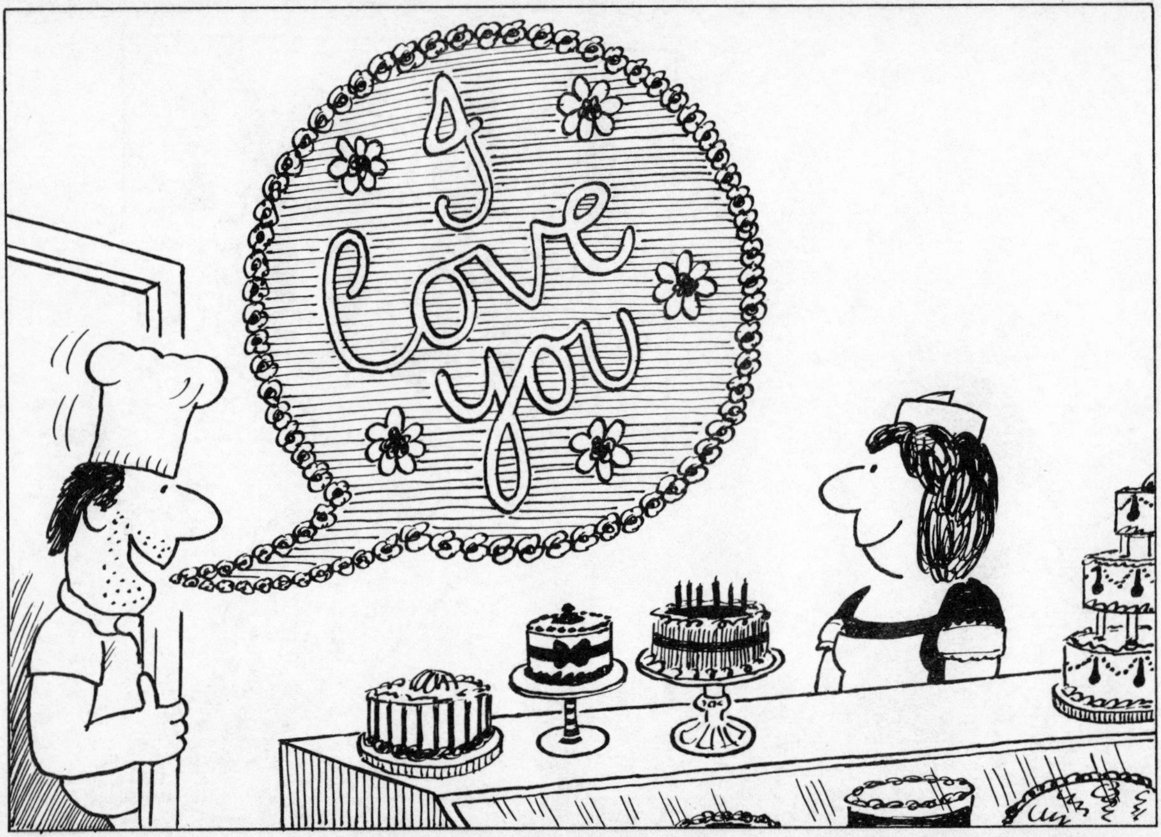
I Love you

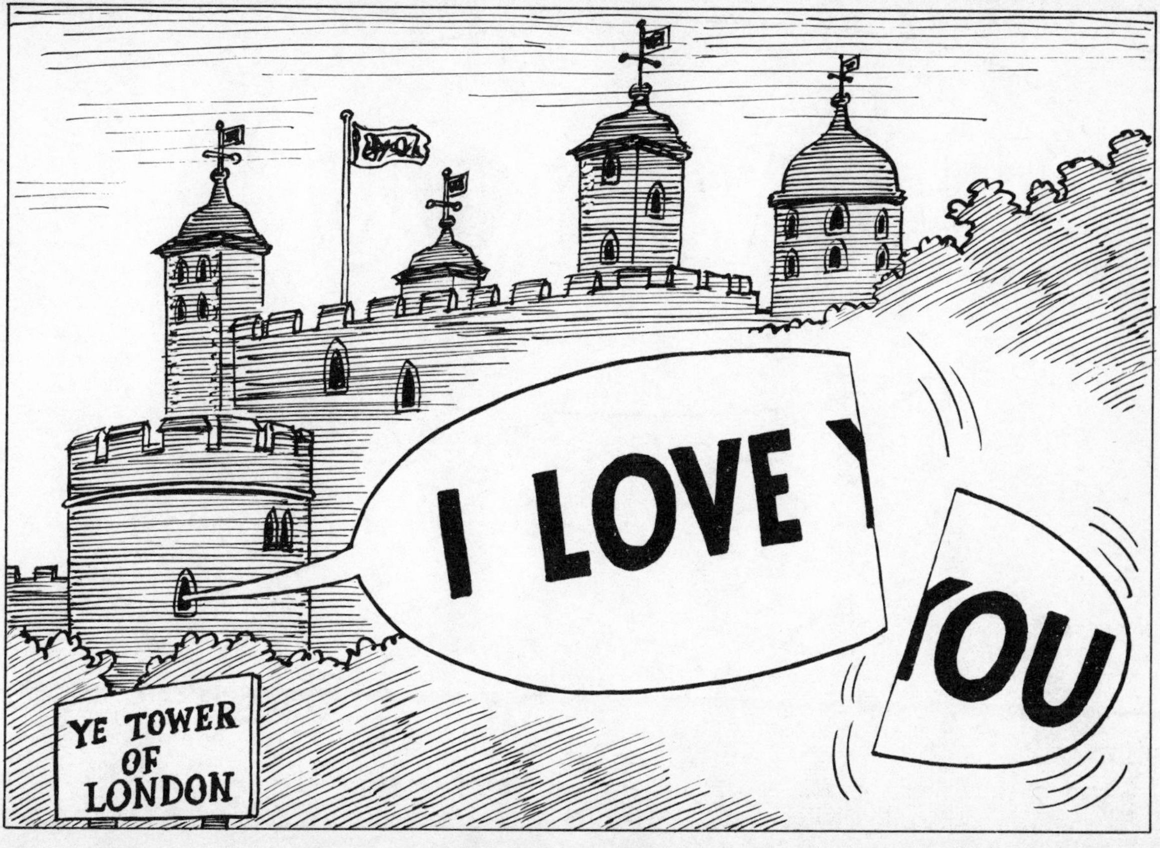
I LOVE Y
YOU
YE TOWER OF LONDON

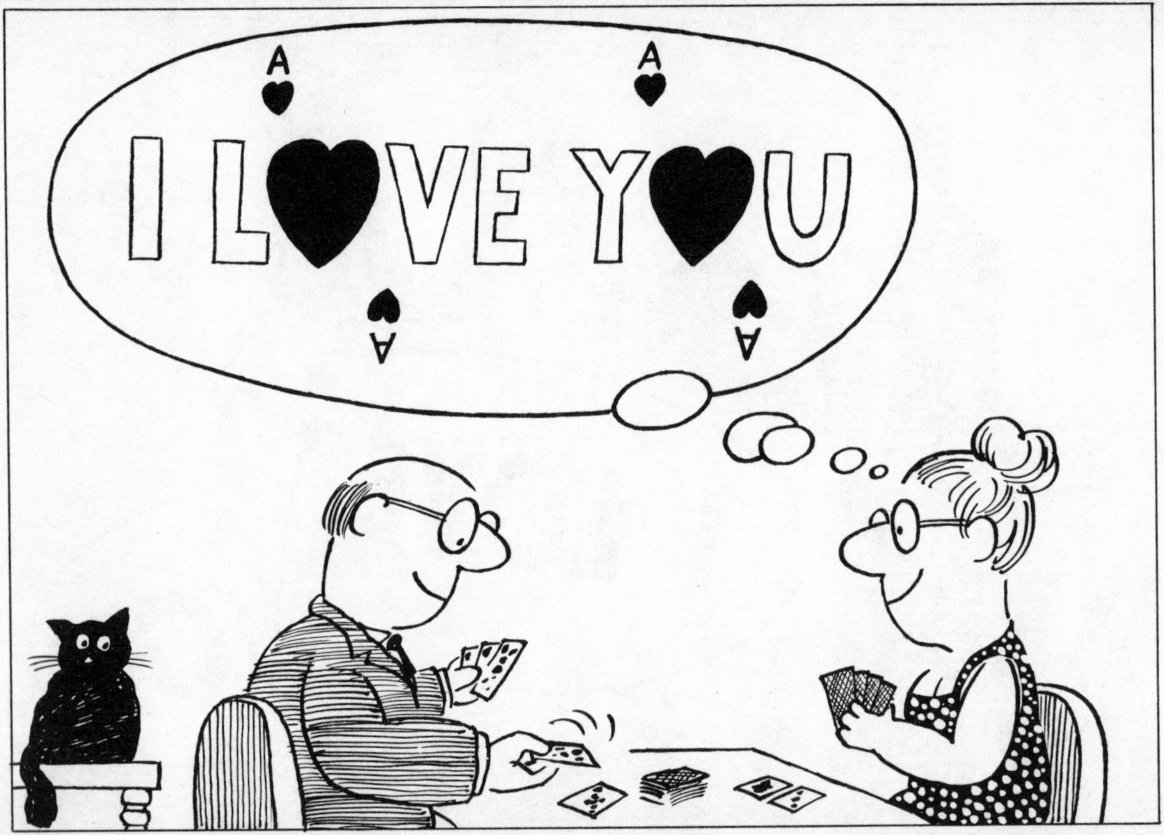
I LOVE YOU

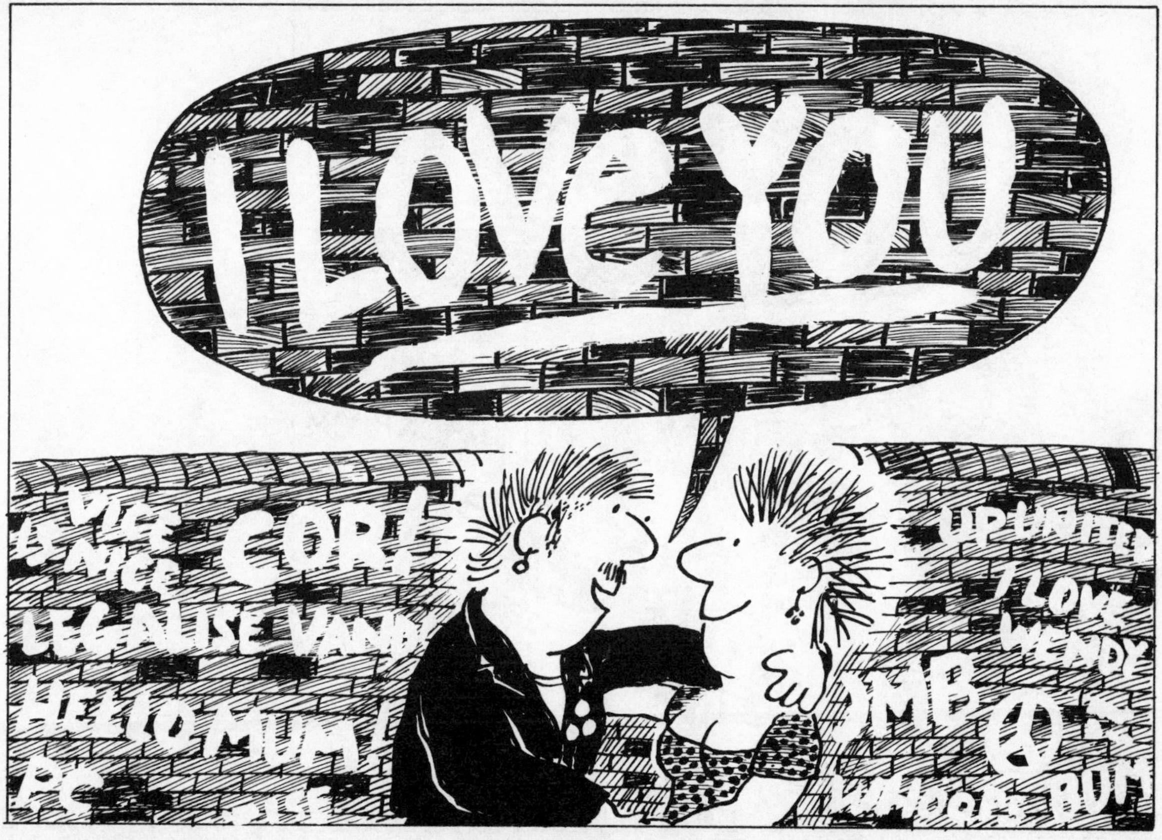
I LOVE YOU
VICE IS NICE
COR!
LEGALISE VAND
HELLO MUM!
PC
UP UNITED
I LOVE WENDY
WHOOPS BUM

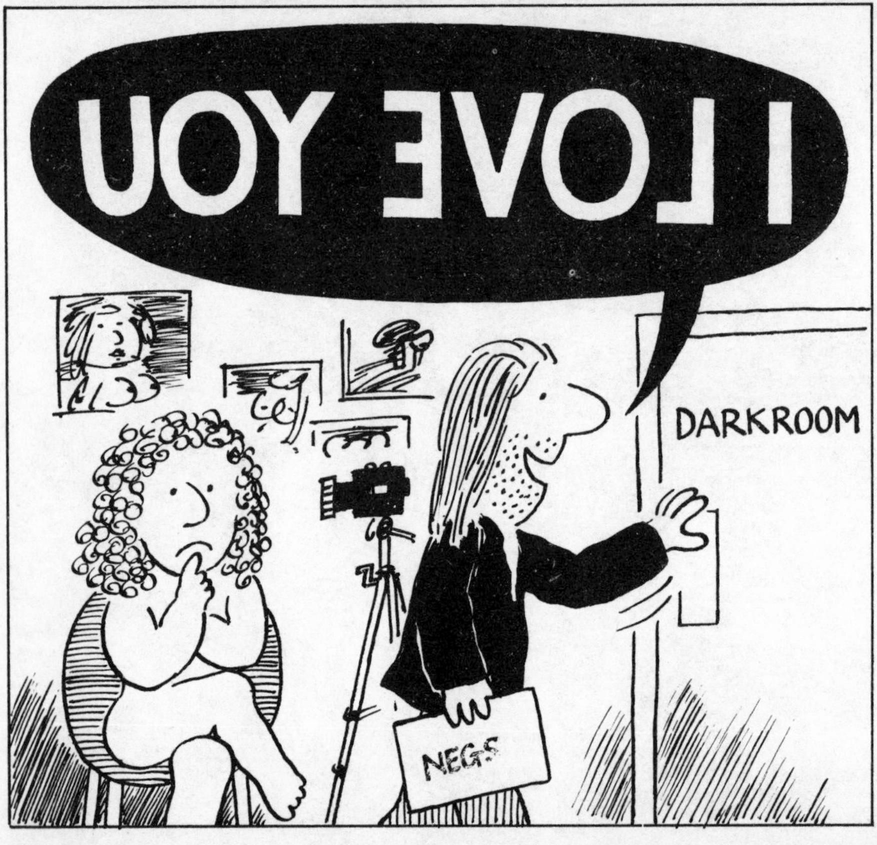
I LOVE YOU
DARKROOM
NEGS

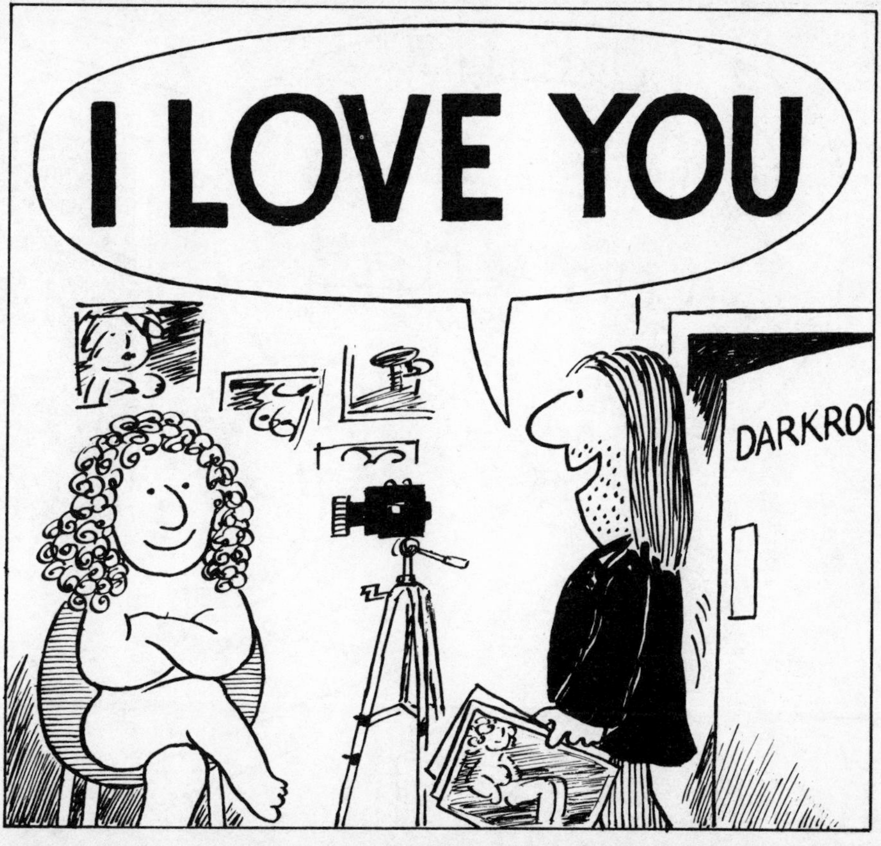
I LOVE YOU
DARKRO

....

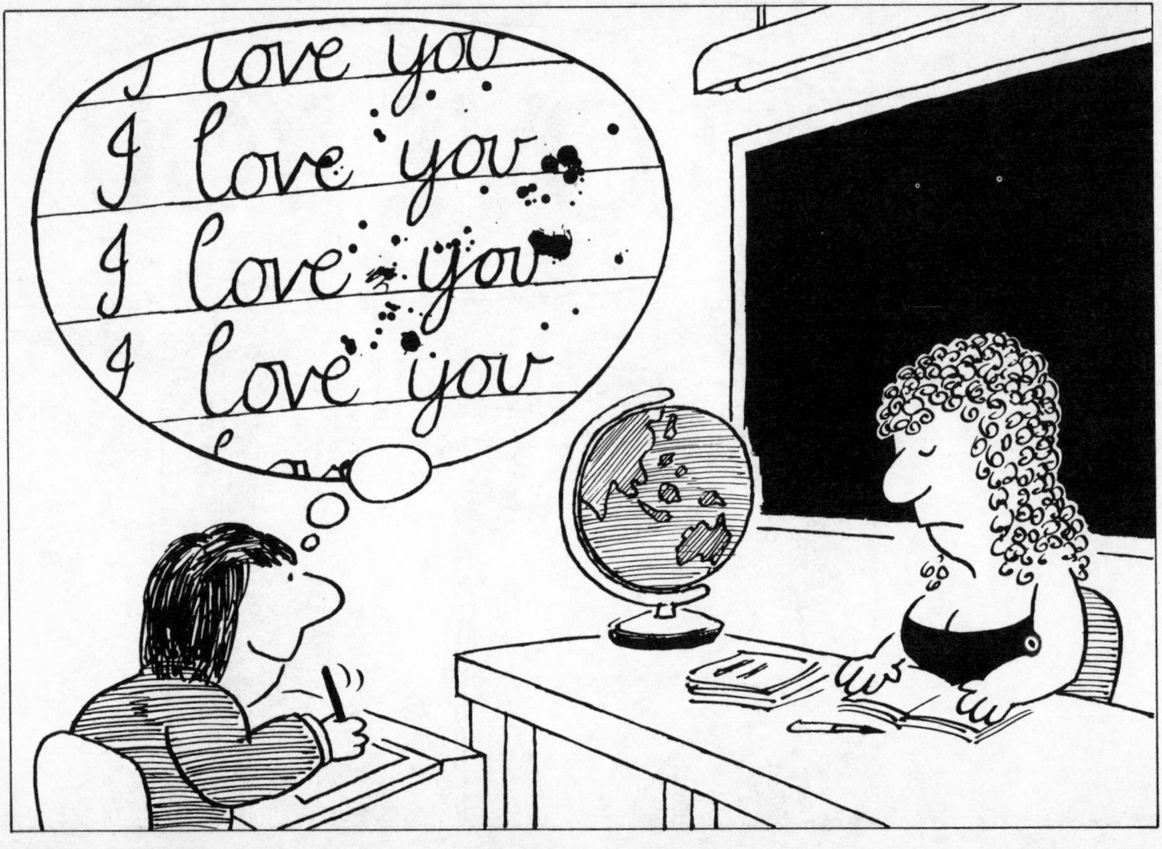
I love you
I love you
I love you
I love you

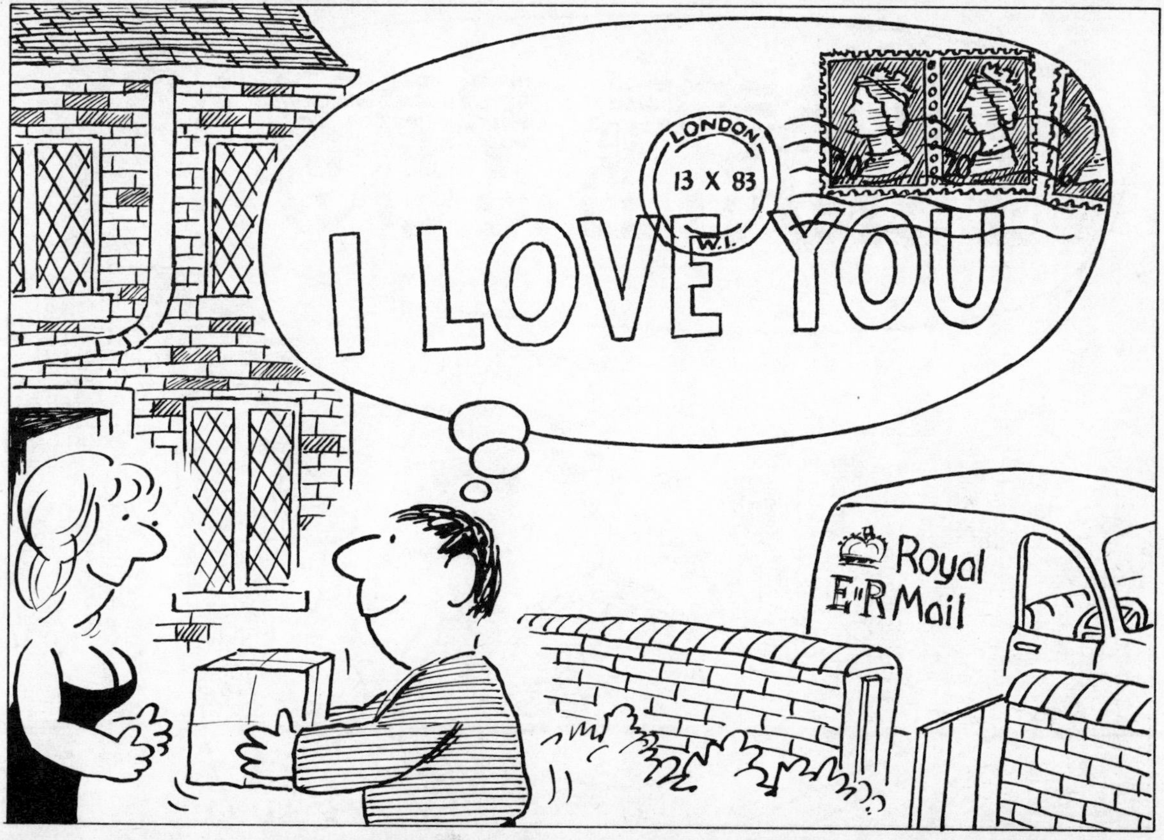

LONDON
13 X 83
W.1.
I LOVE YOU
Royal
E R Mail

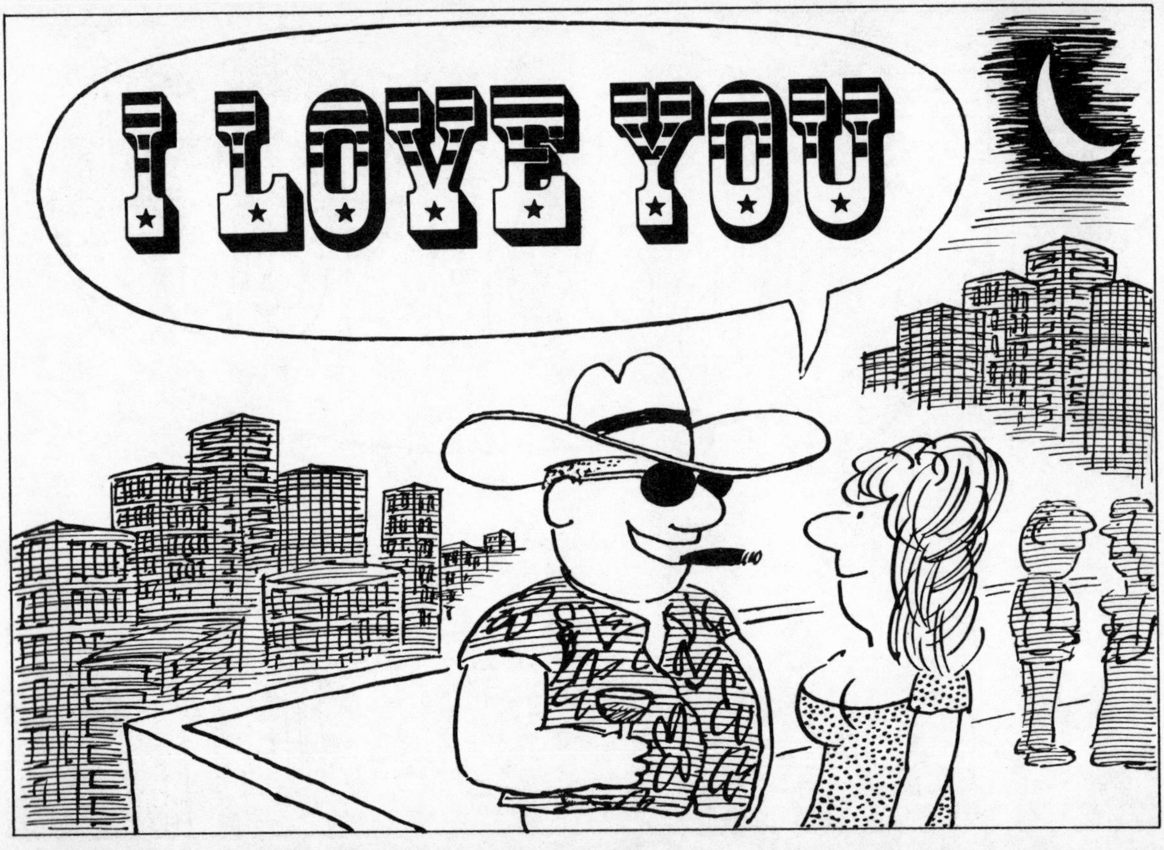
I LOVE YOU

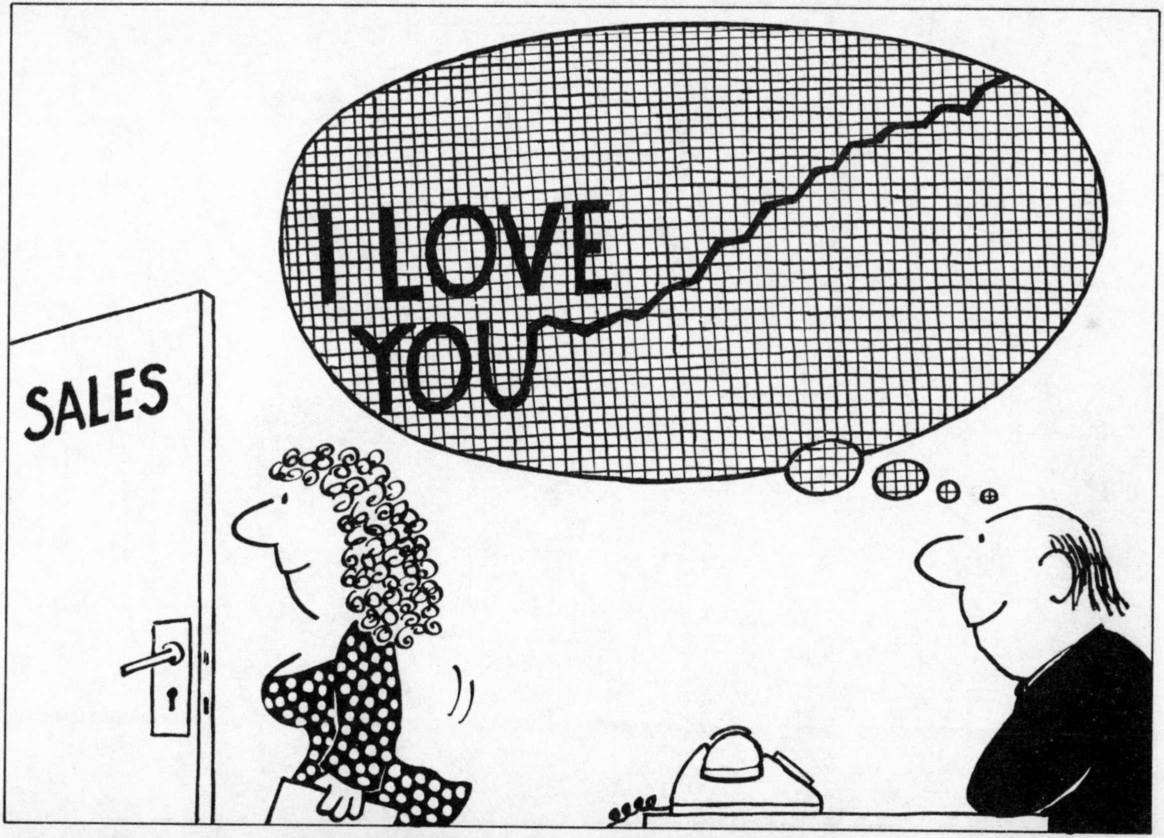
SALES
I LOVE YOU

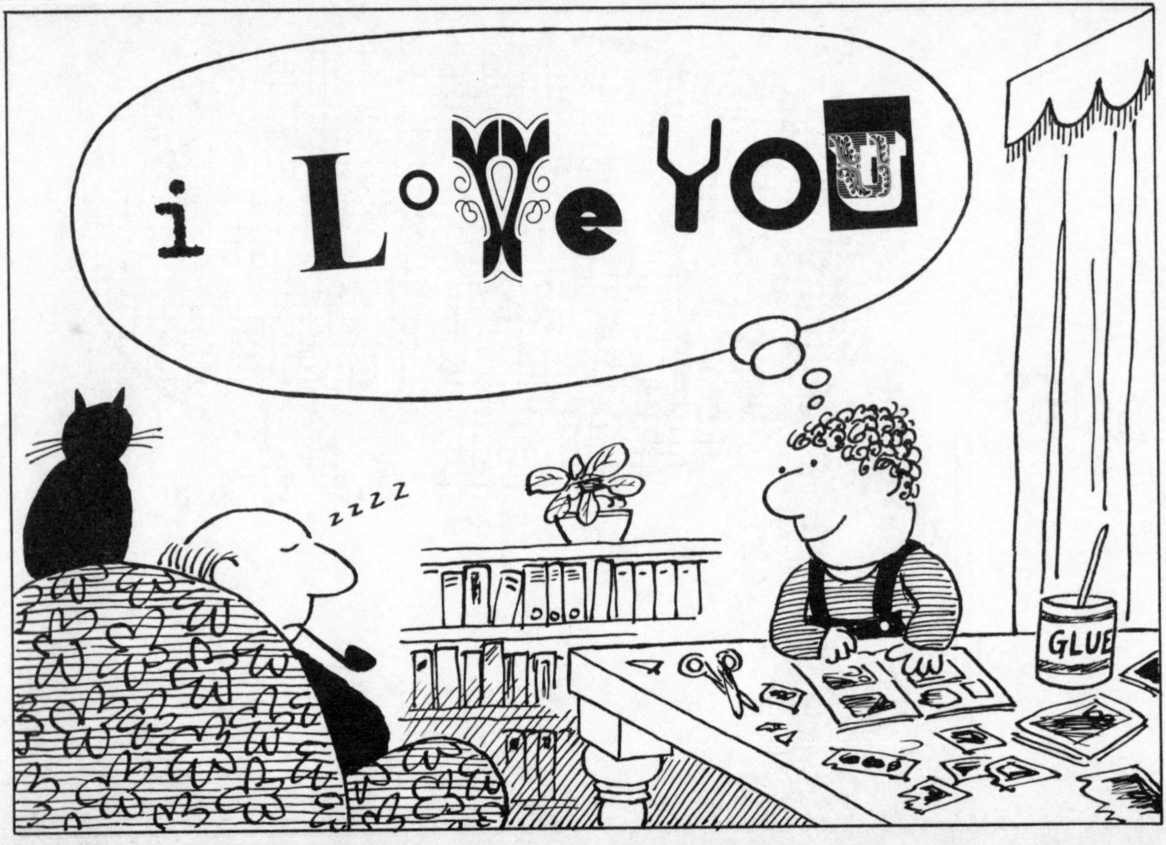

i LOVe YOU
ZZZZ
GLUE

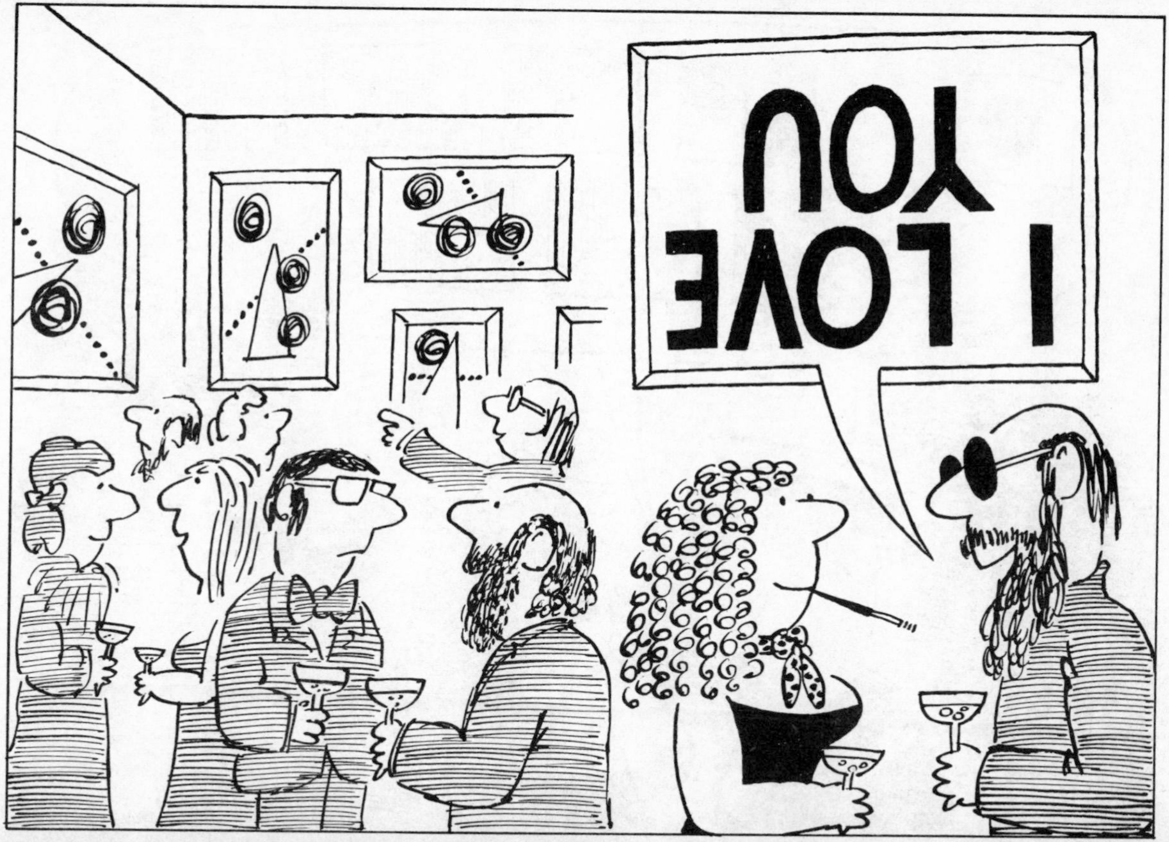
I LOVE
YOU

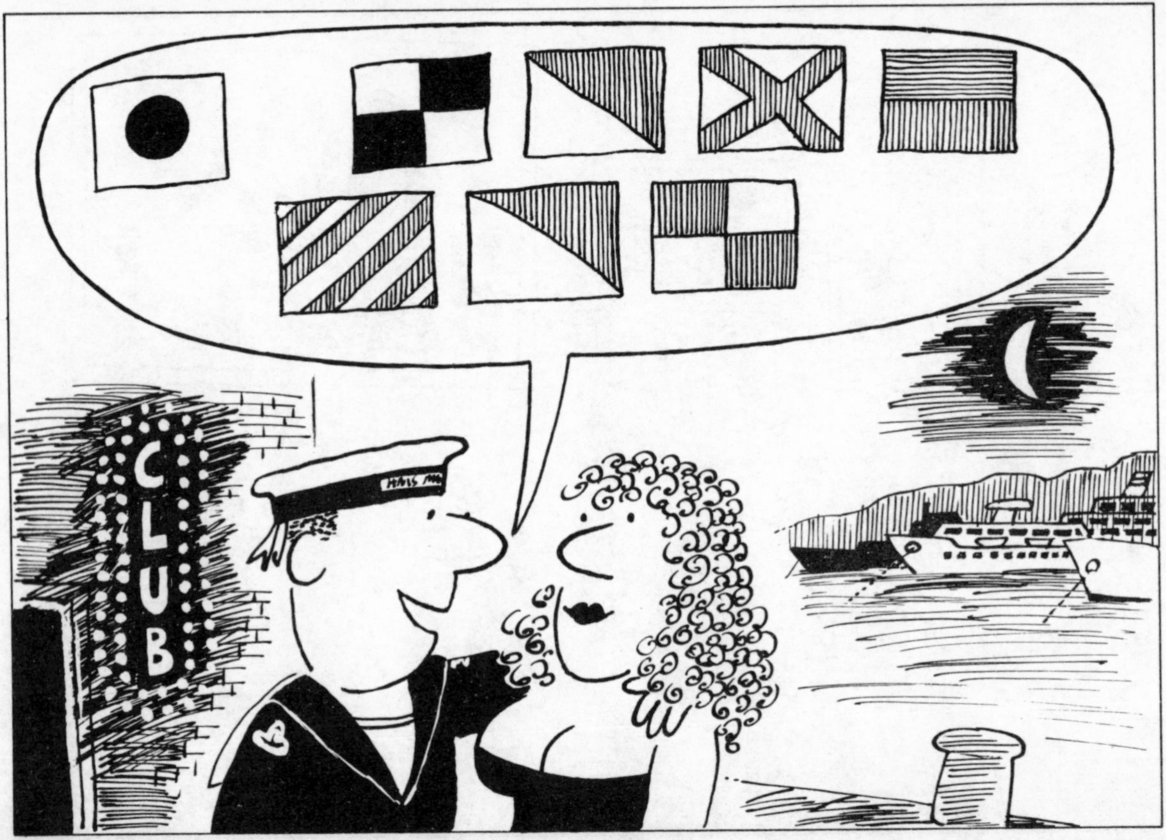
CLUB

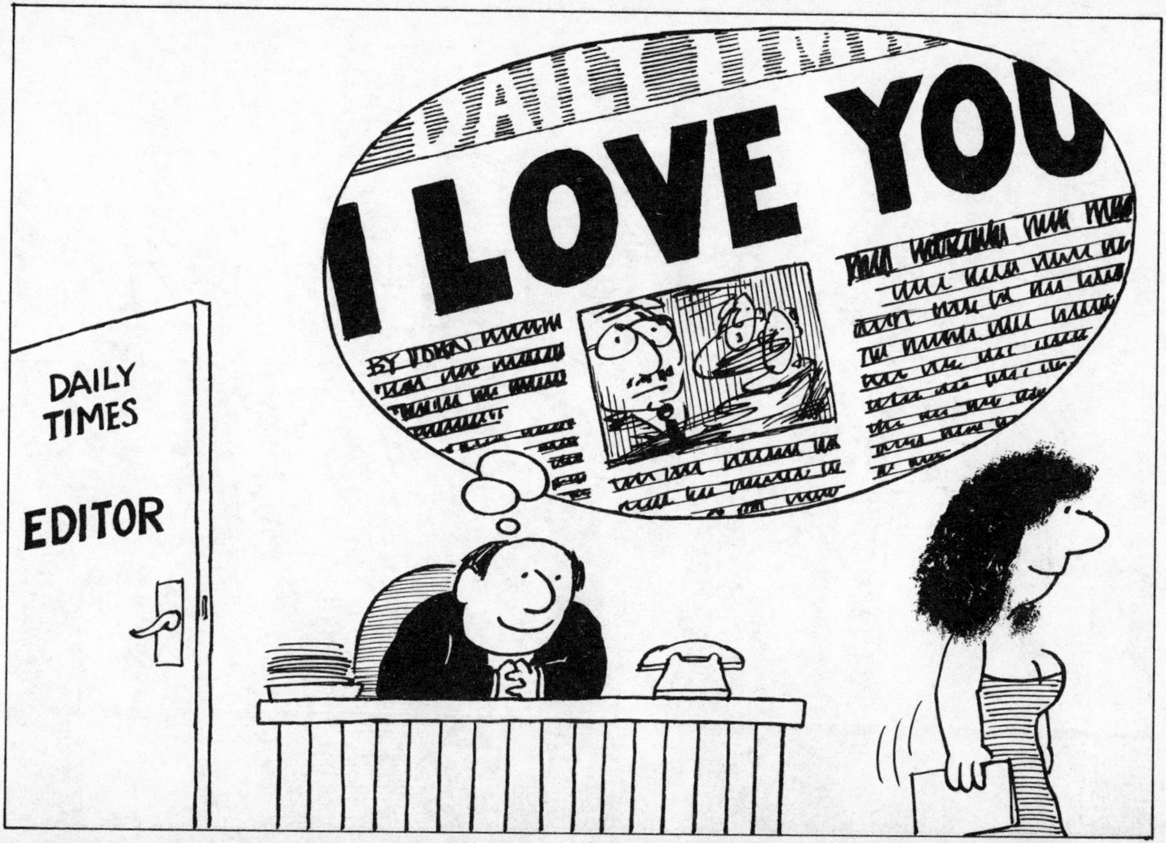
I LOVE YOU
DAILY TIMES
EDITOR

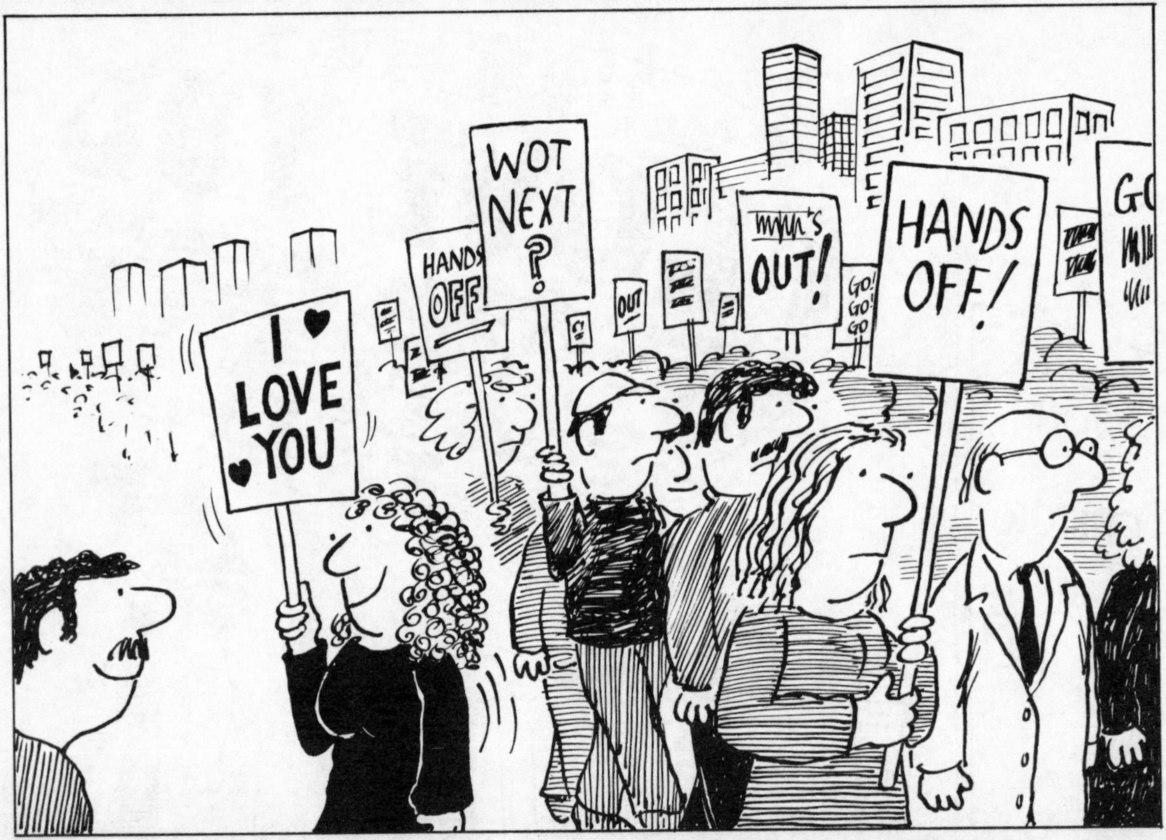
I LOVE YOU
HANDS OFF
WOT NEXT ?
OUT
'S OUT!
GO! GO! GO
HANDS OFF!

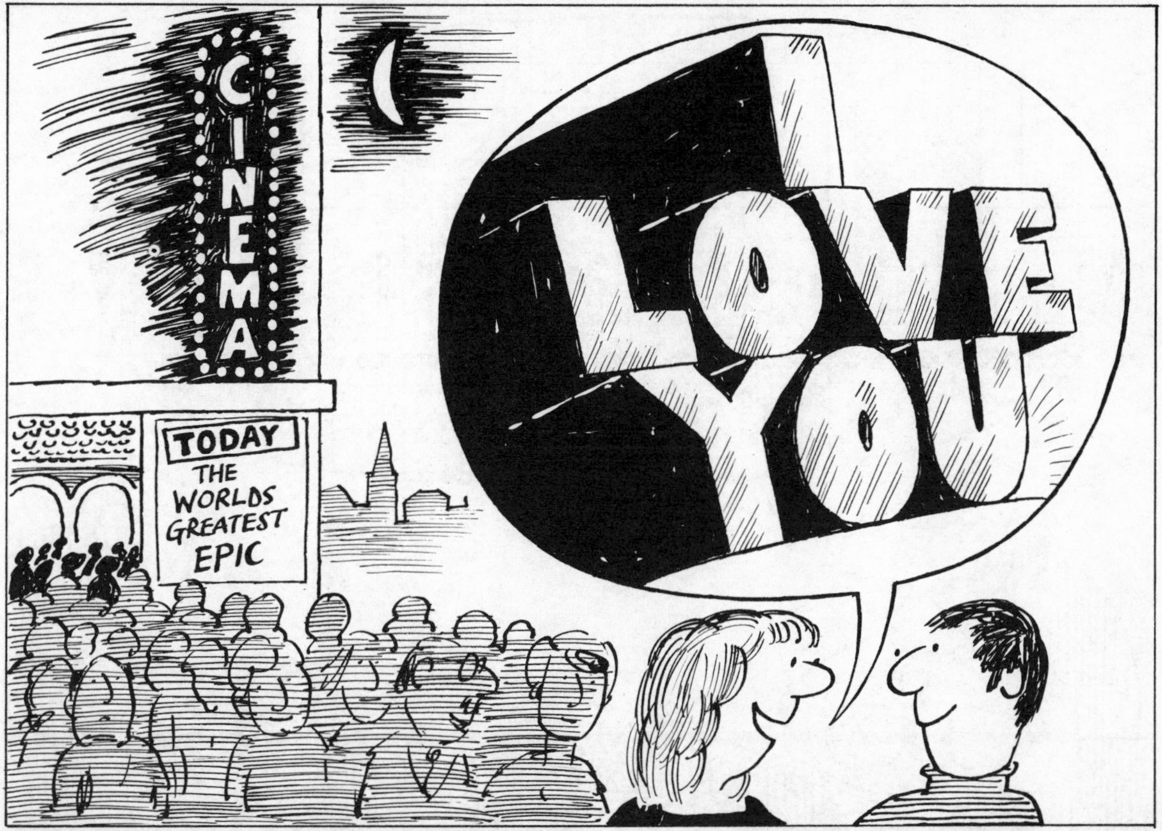
CINEMA
TODAY
THE WORLDS GREATEST EPIC
I LOVE YOU

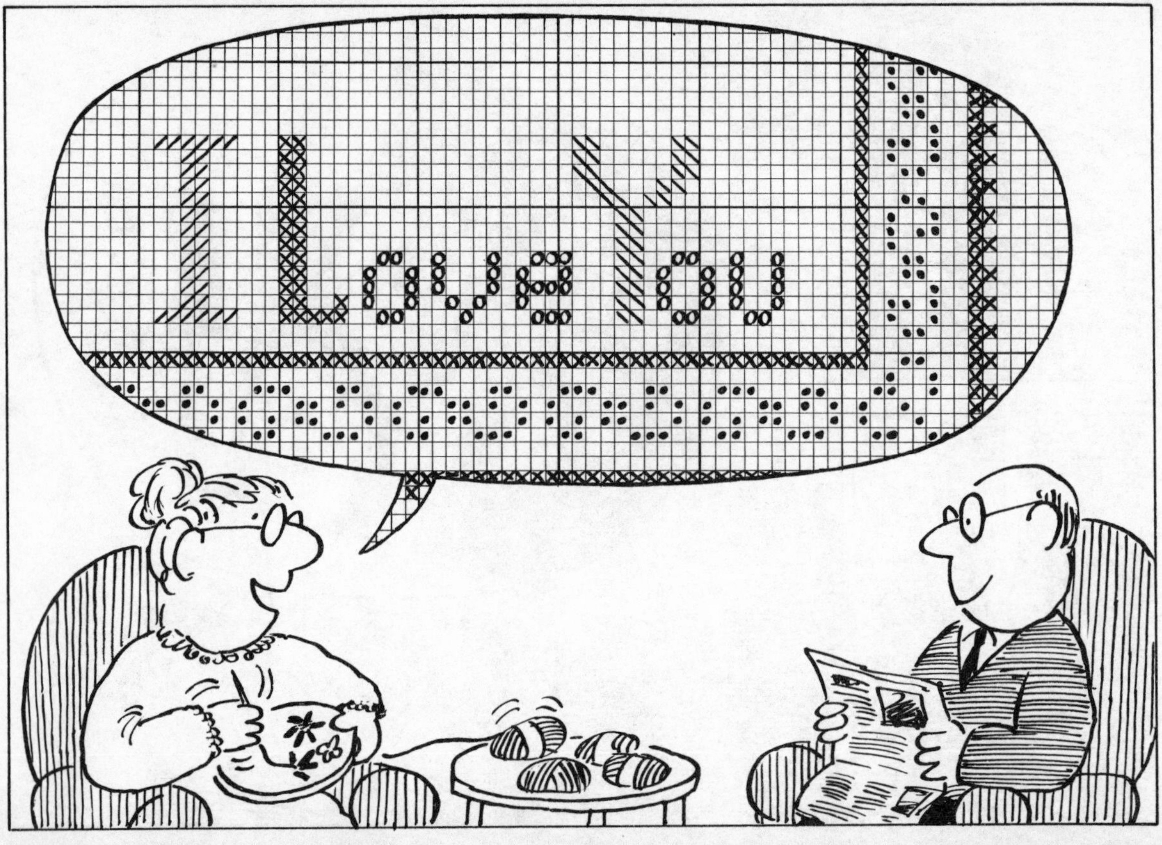
I Love You

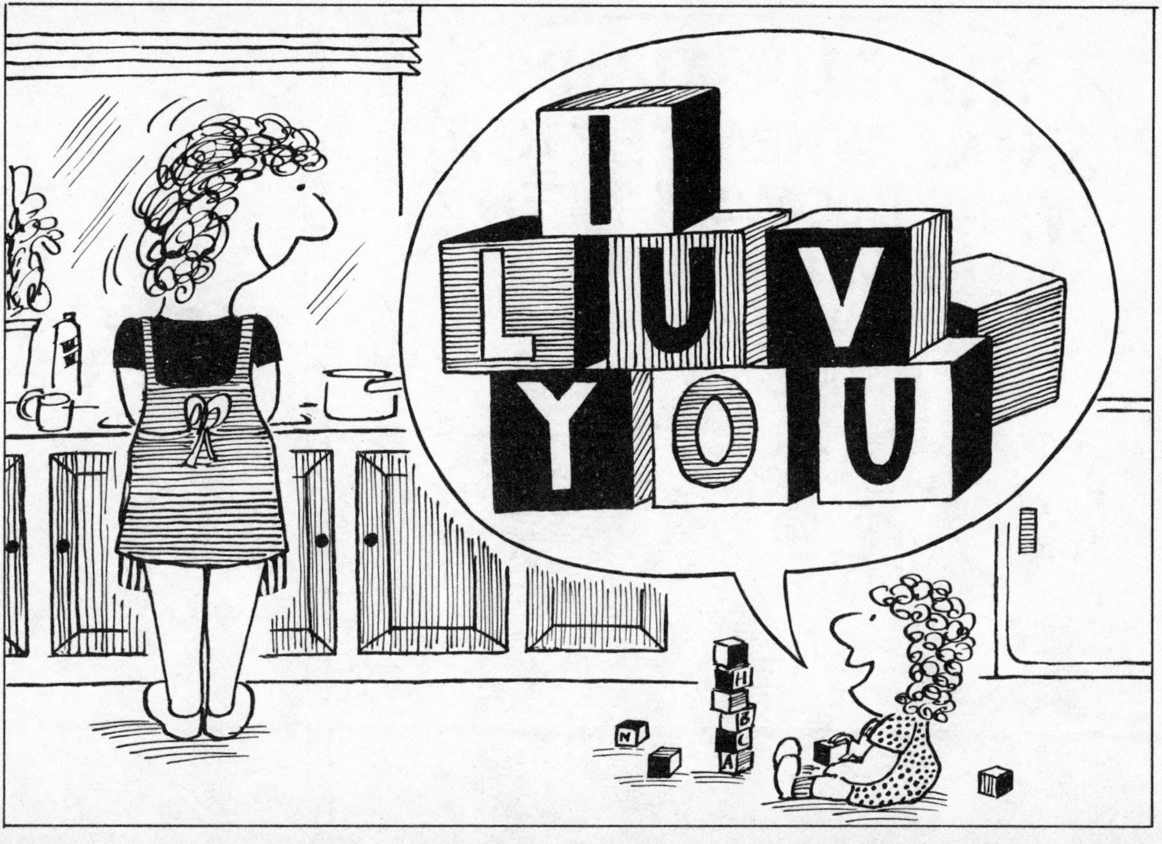
I LUV YOU

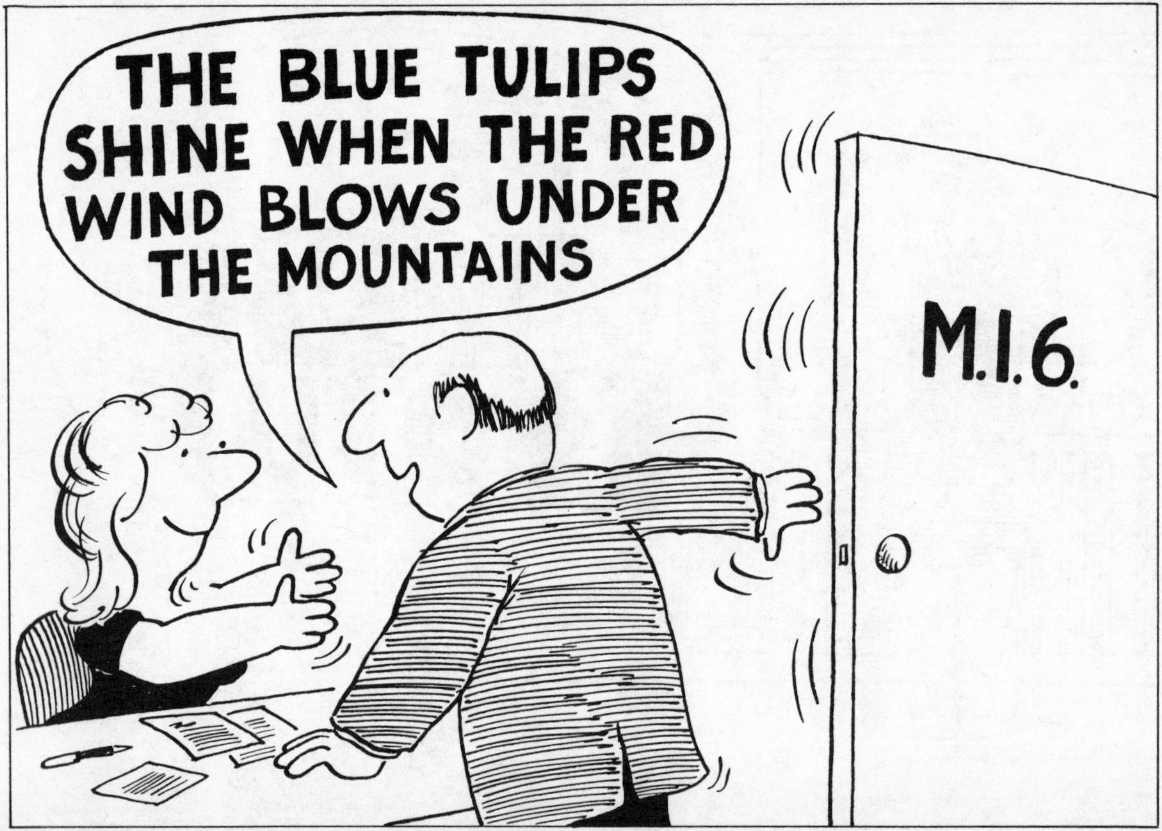
THE BLUE TULIPS SHINE WHEN THE RED WIND BLOWS UNDER THE MOUNTAINS
M.I.6.

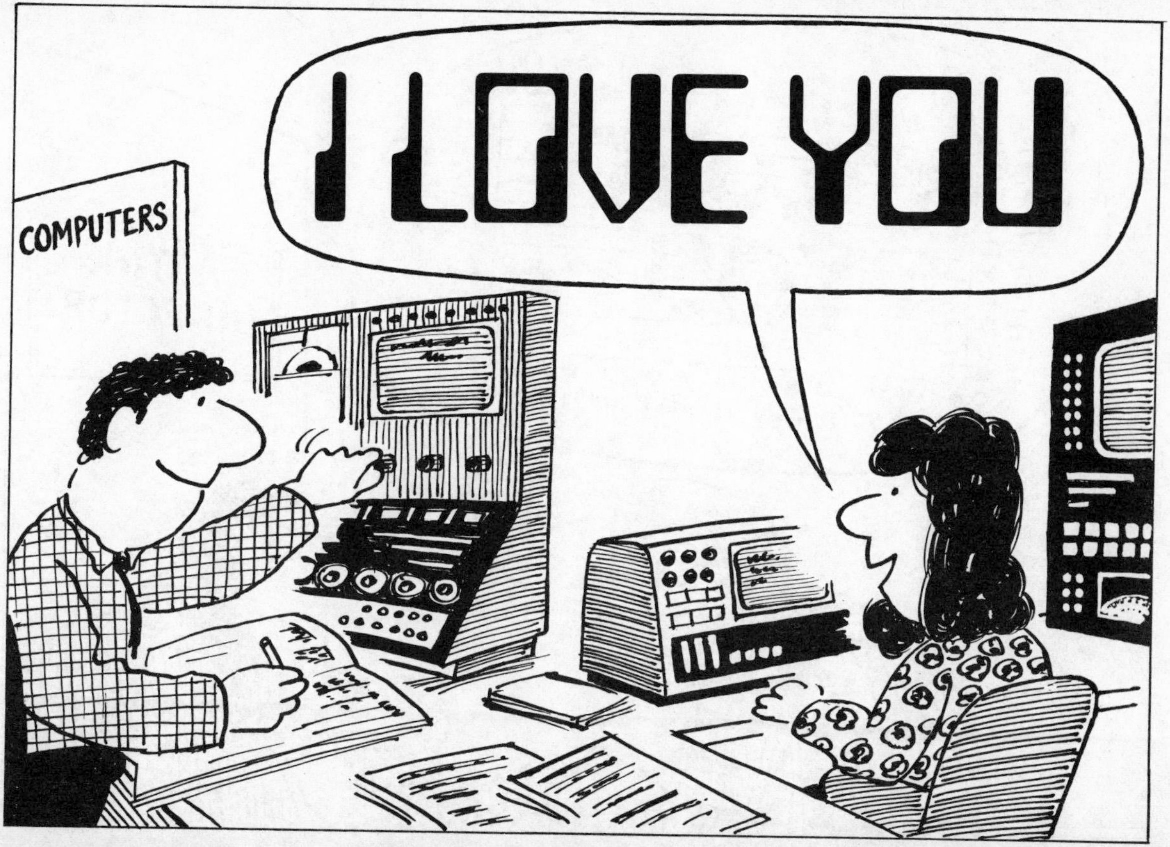
COMPUTERS
I LOVE YOU

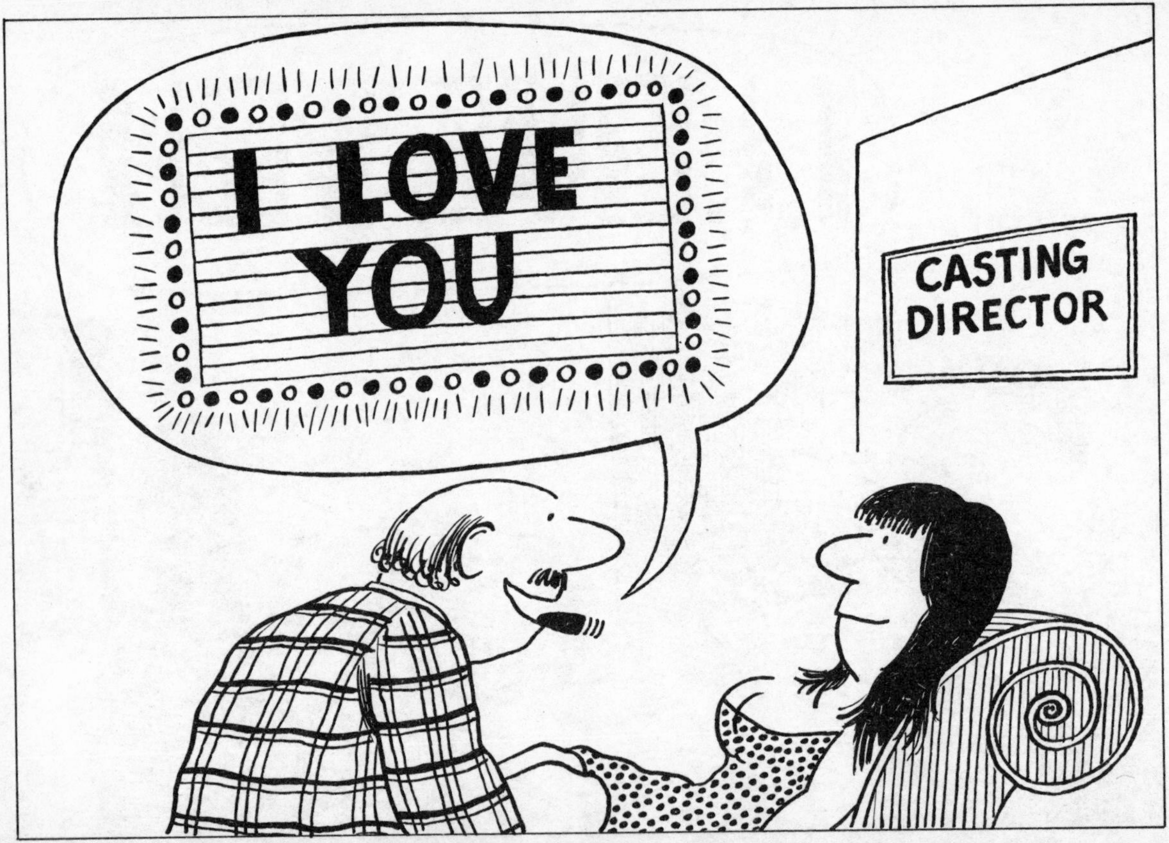
I LOVE YOU
CASTING DIRECTOR

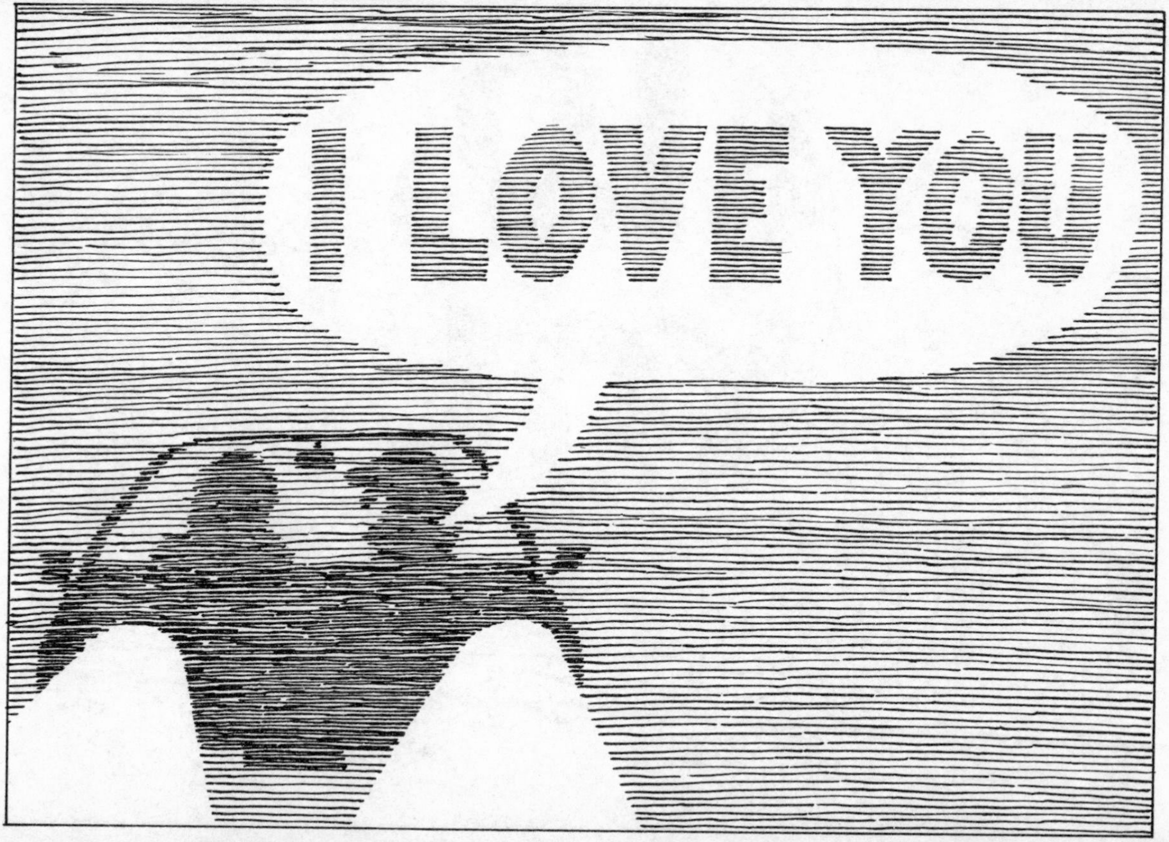
I LOVE YOU

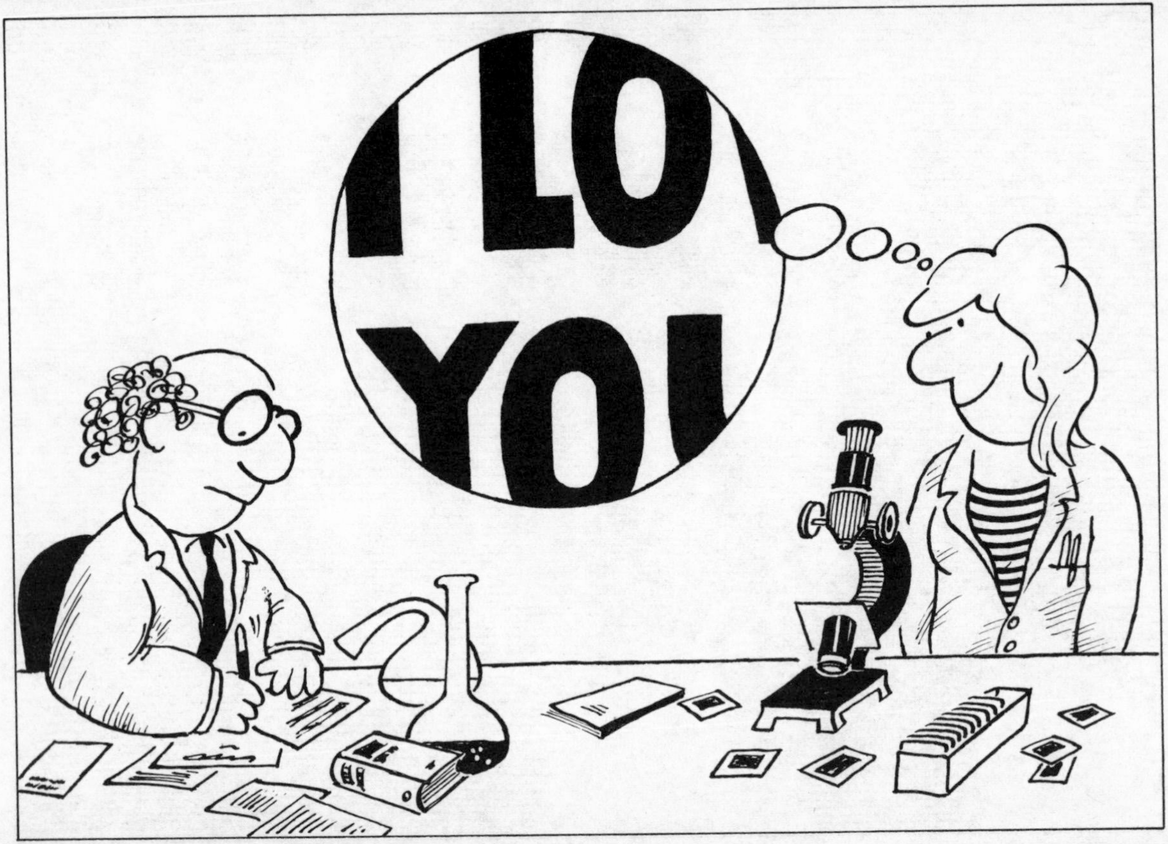
I LO
YO

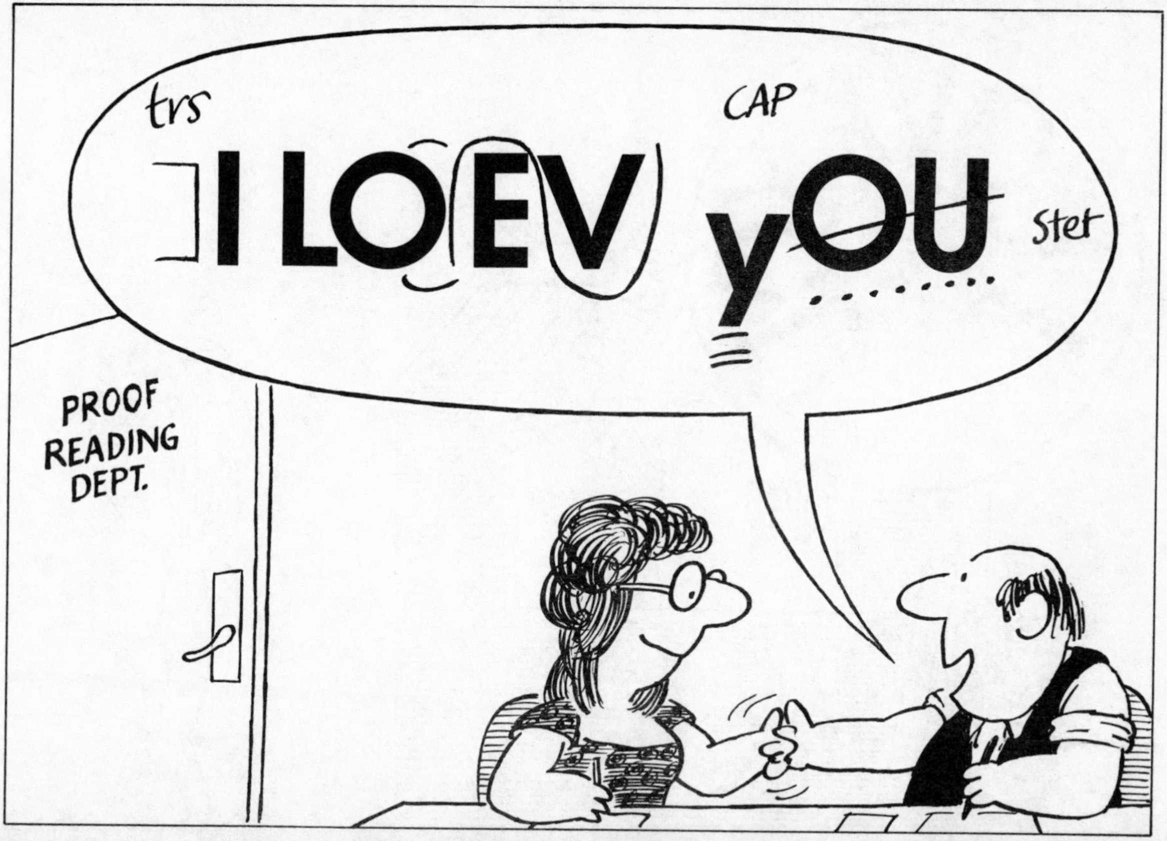

trs
CAP
I LOEV yOU
Stet
PROOF
READING
DEPT.

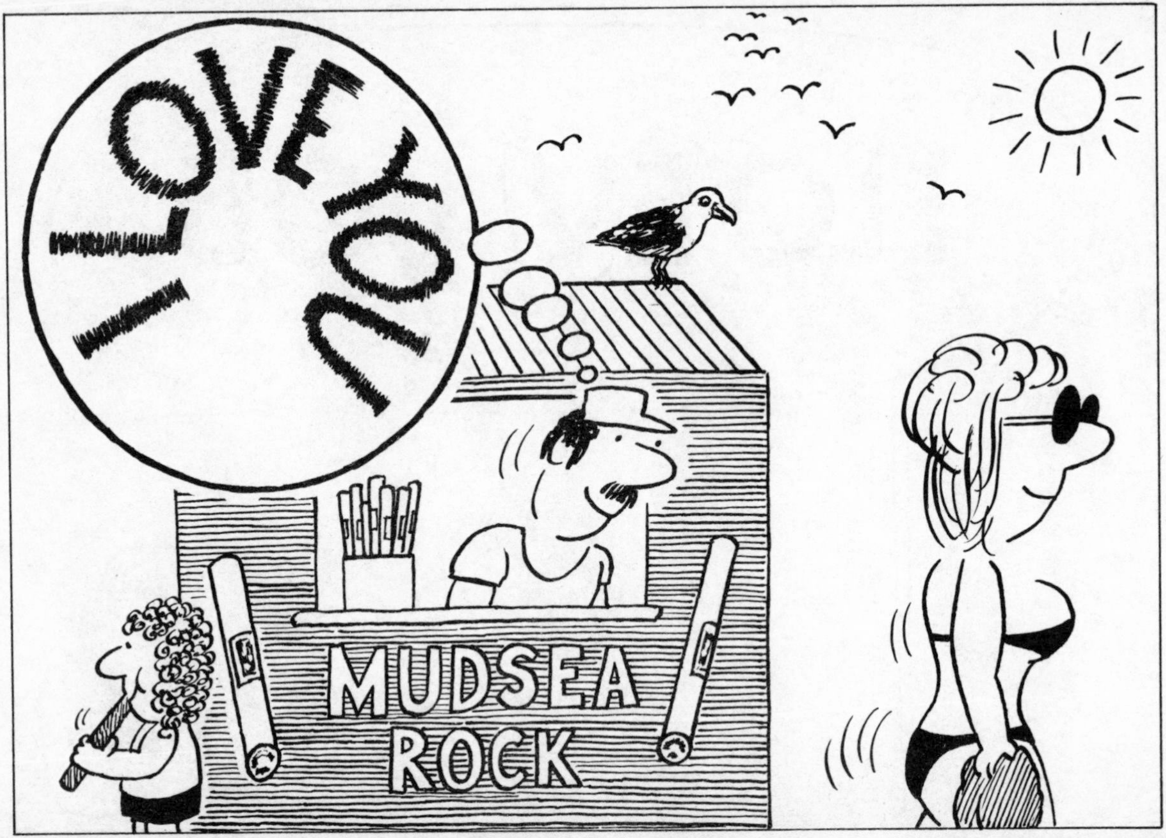
I LOVE YOU
MUDSEA
ROCK

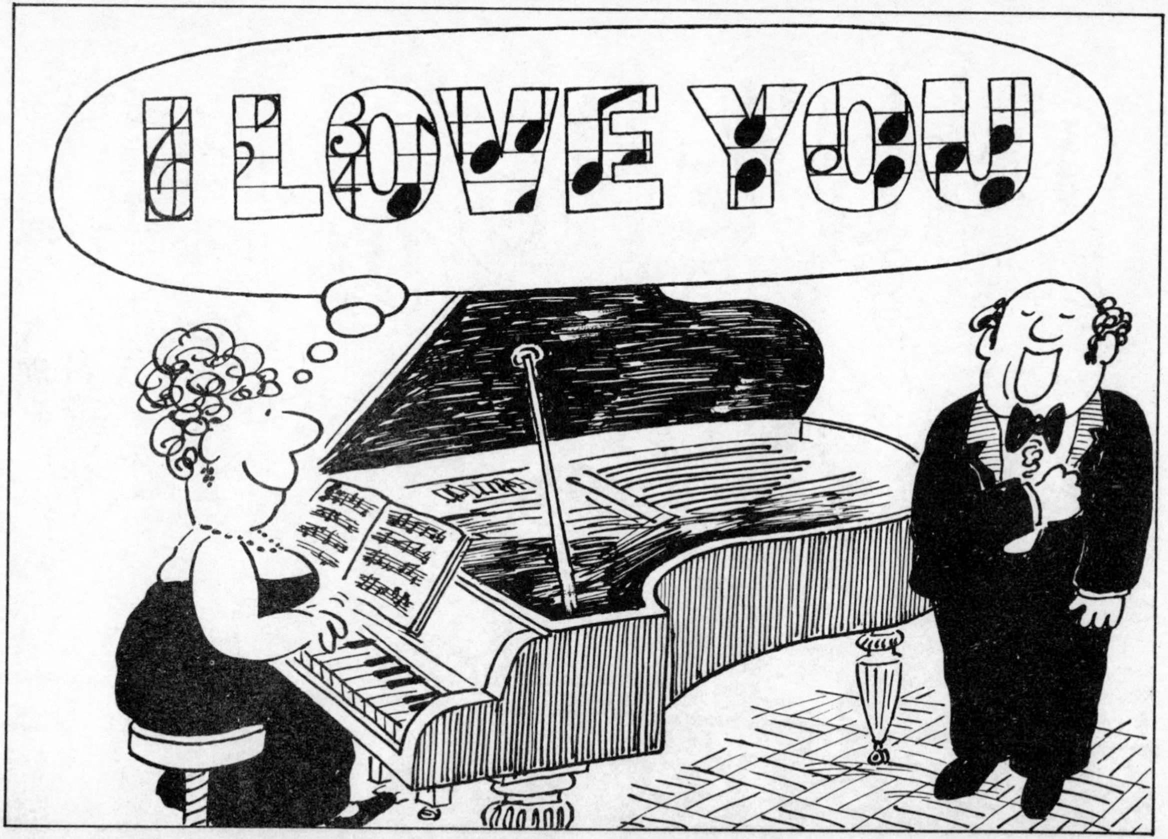
I LOVE YOU

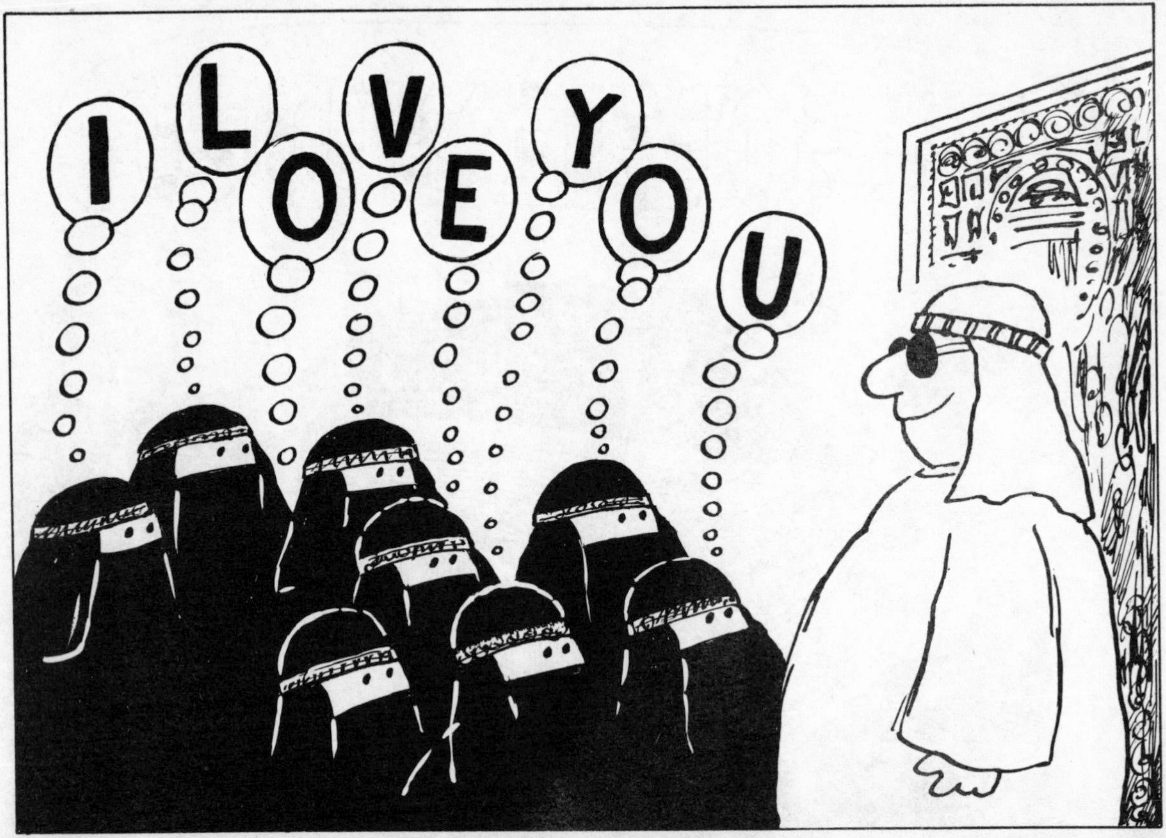
I
L
O
V
E
Y
O
U

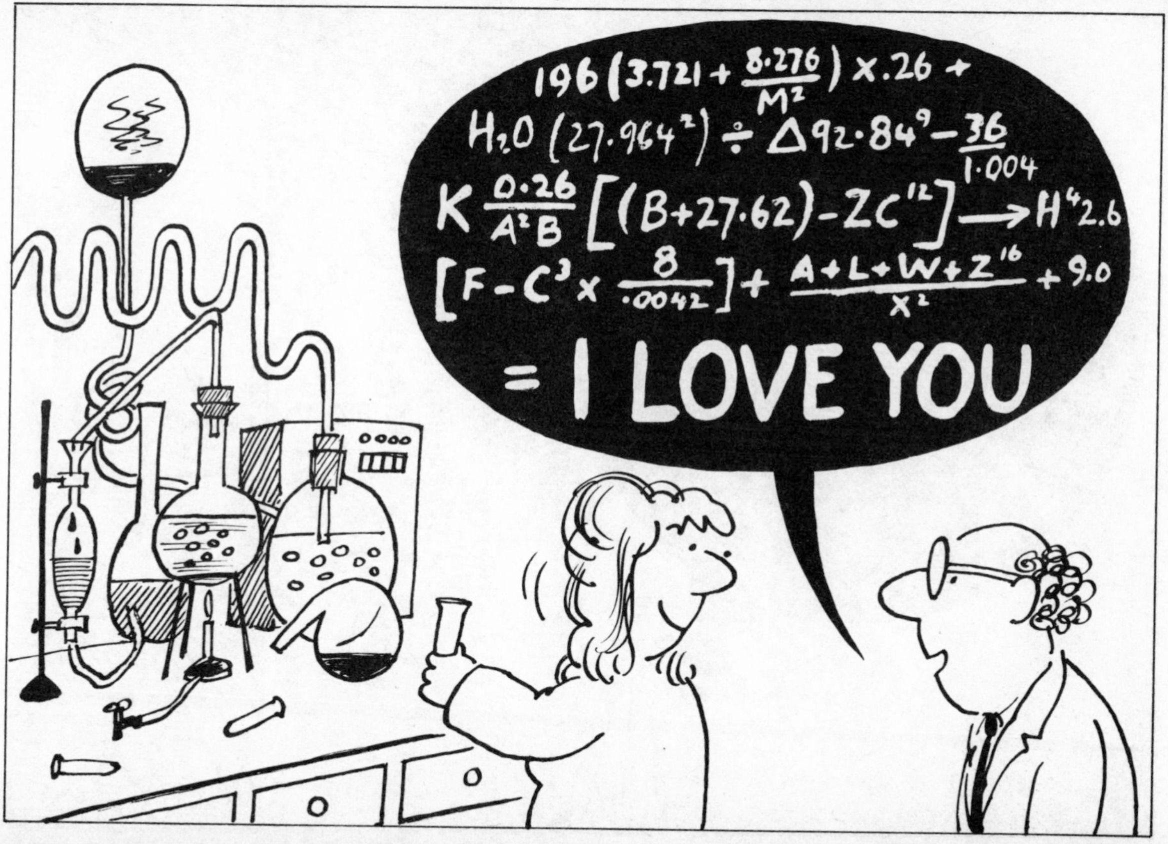
196 (3.721 + 8·276/M²) x.26 +
H₂O (27·964²) ÷ Δ92·84⁹ − 36/1·004
K 0·26/A²B [(B+27·62)−ZC¹²] → H⁴2.6
[F−C³ x 8/·0042] + (A+L+W+Z¹⁶)/X² + 9.0
= I LOVE YOU

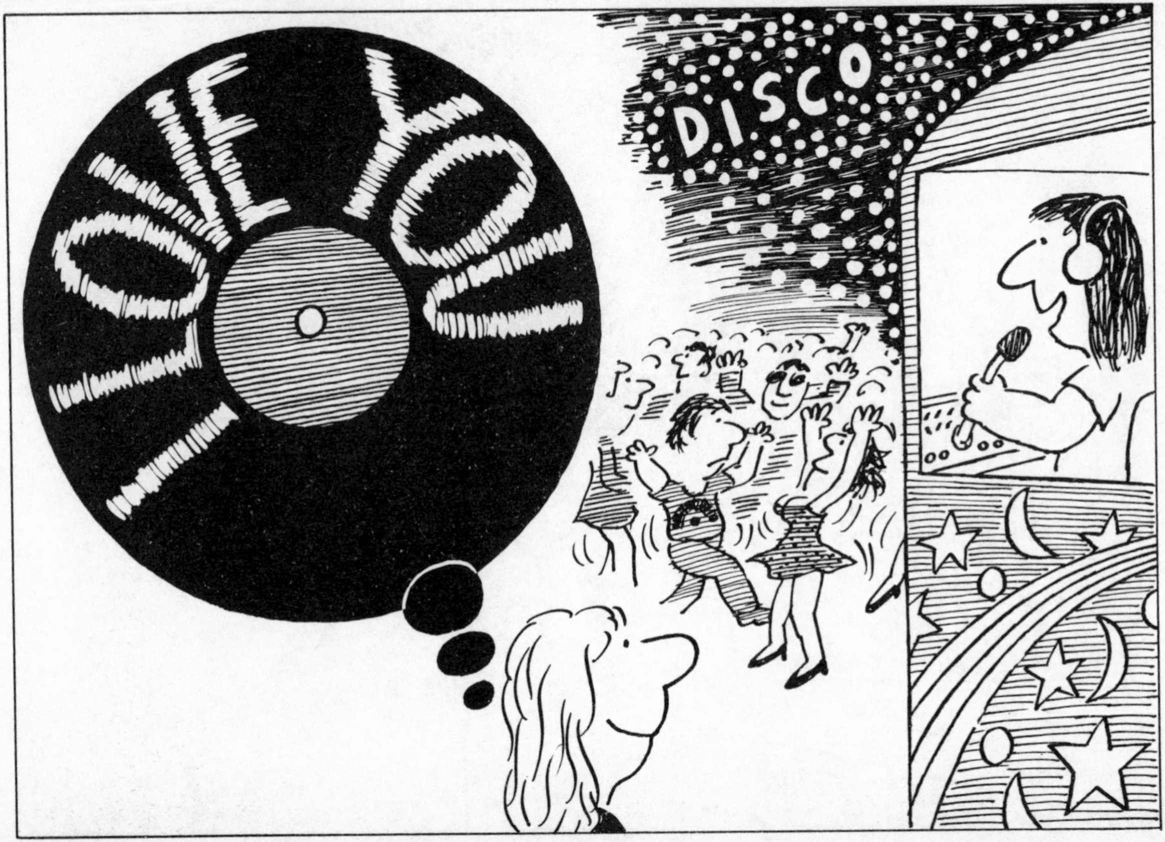
I LOVE YOU
DISCO

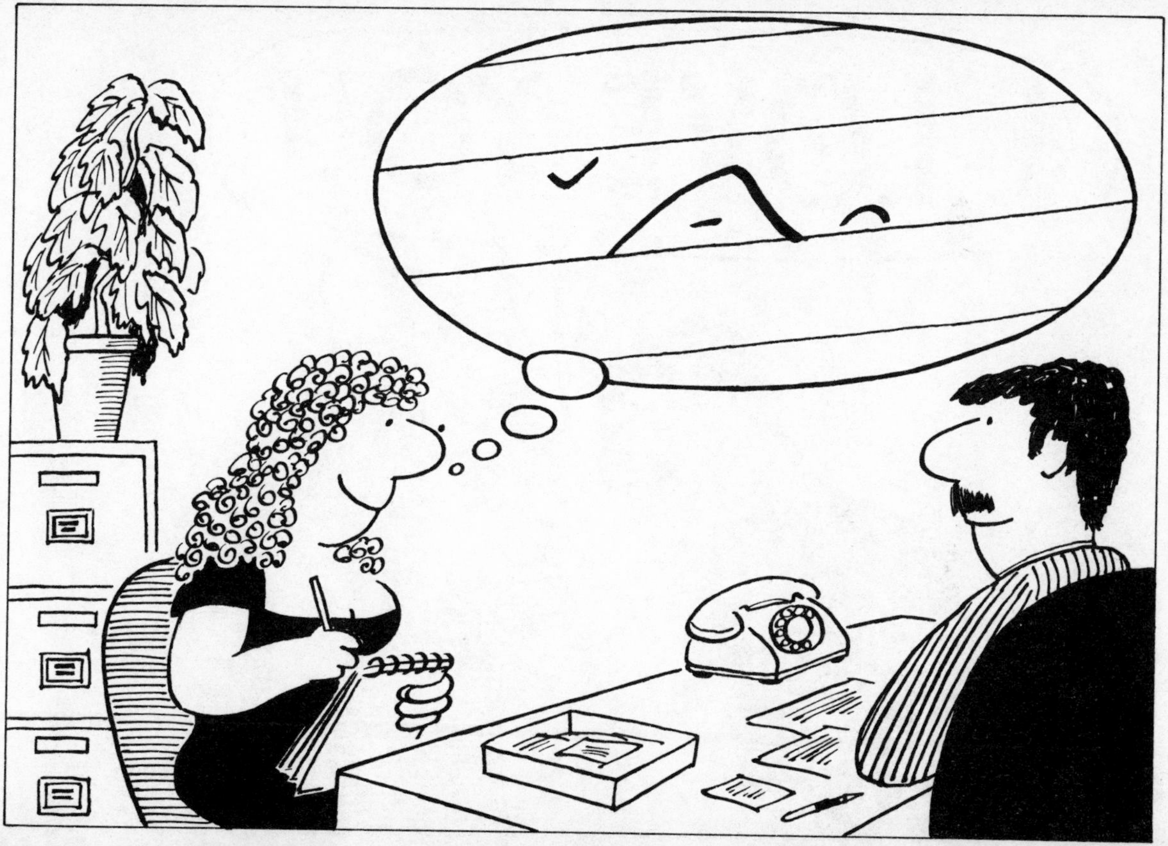

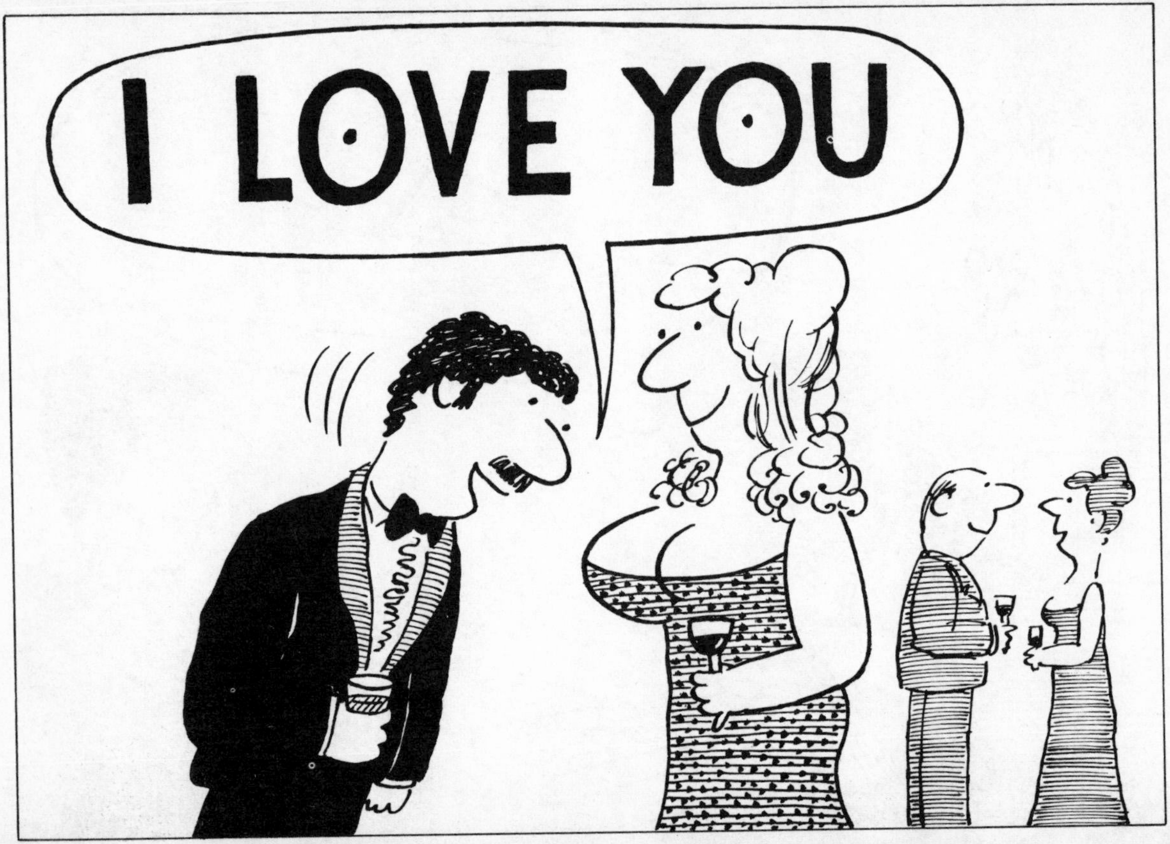
I LOVE YOU

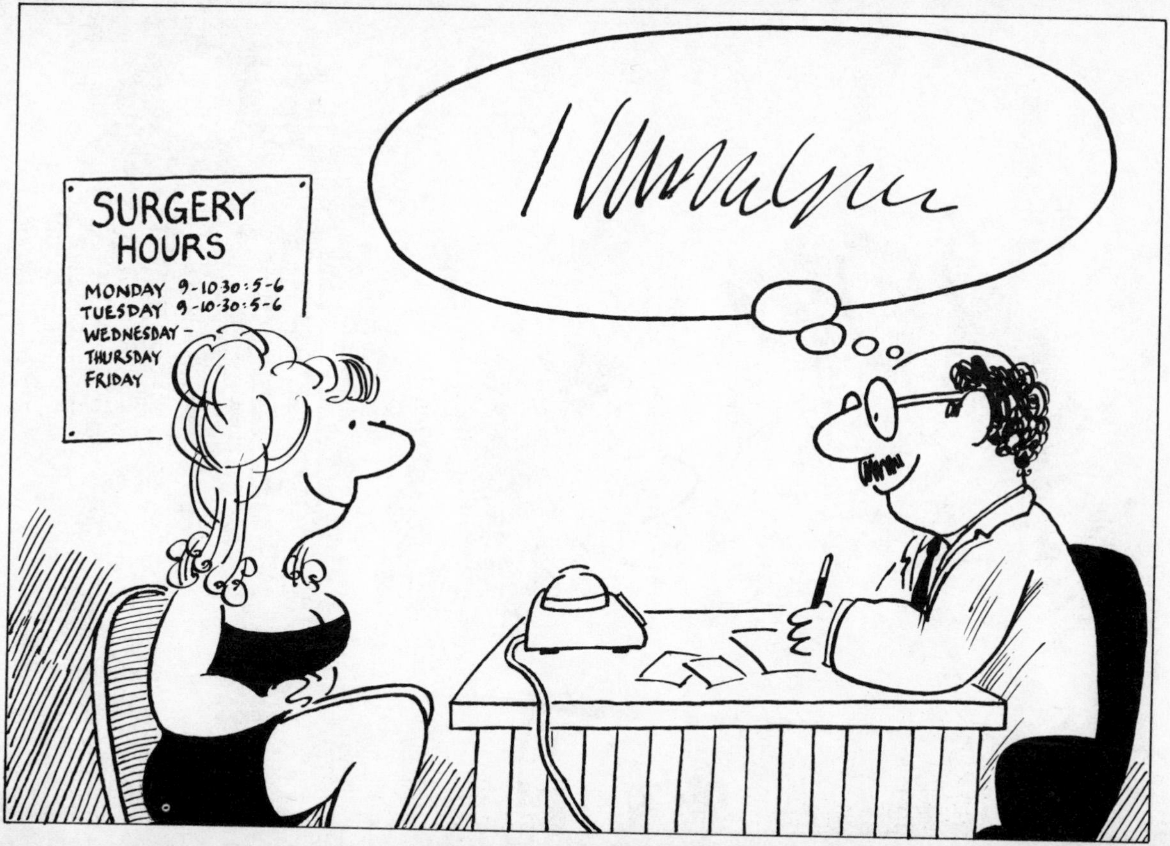

SURGERY HOURS
MONDAY 9-10·30 : 5-6
TUESDAY 9-10·30 : 5-6
WEDNESDAY -
THURSDAY
FRIDAY

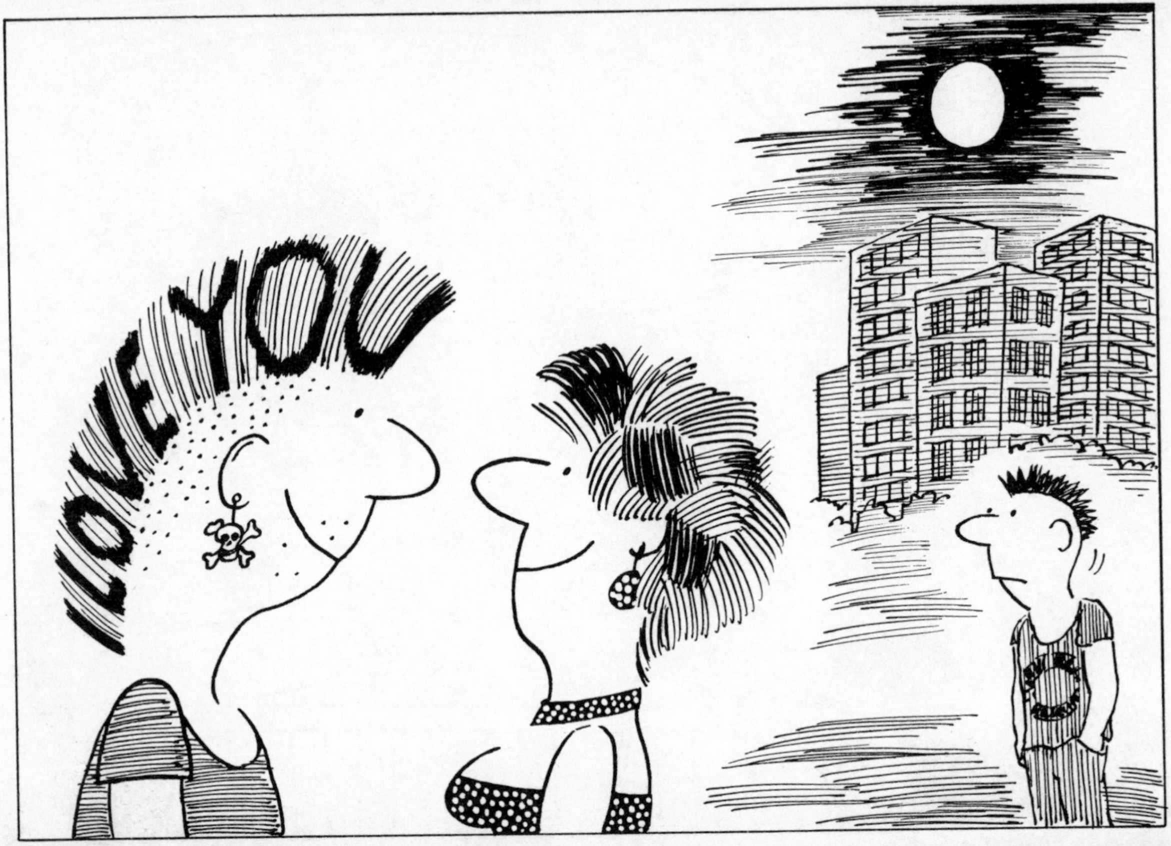
I LOVE YOU

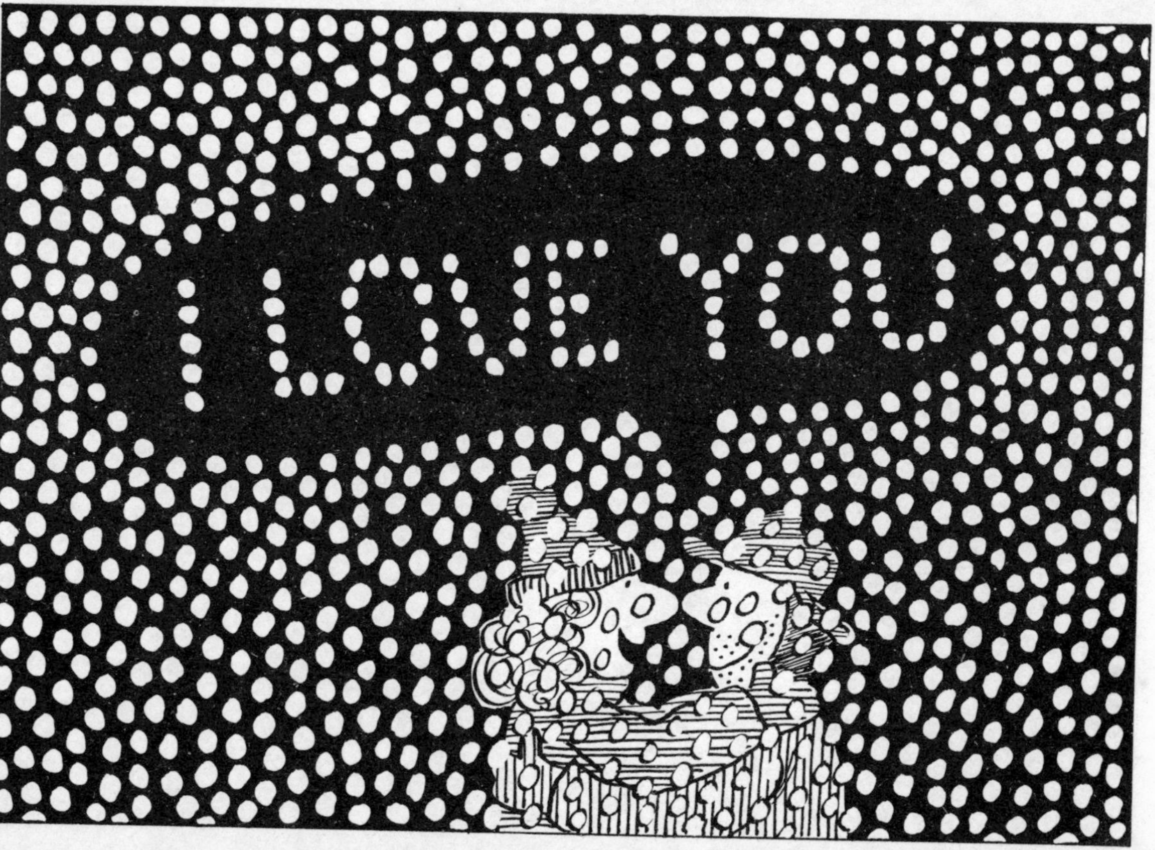
I LOVE YOU

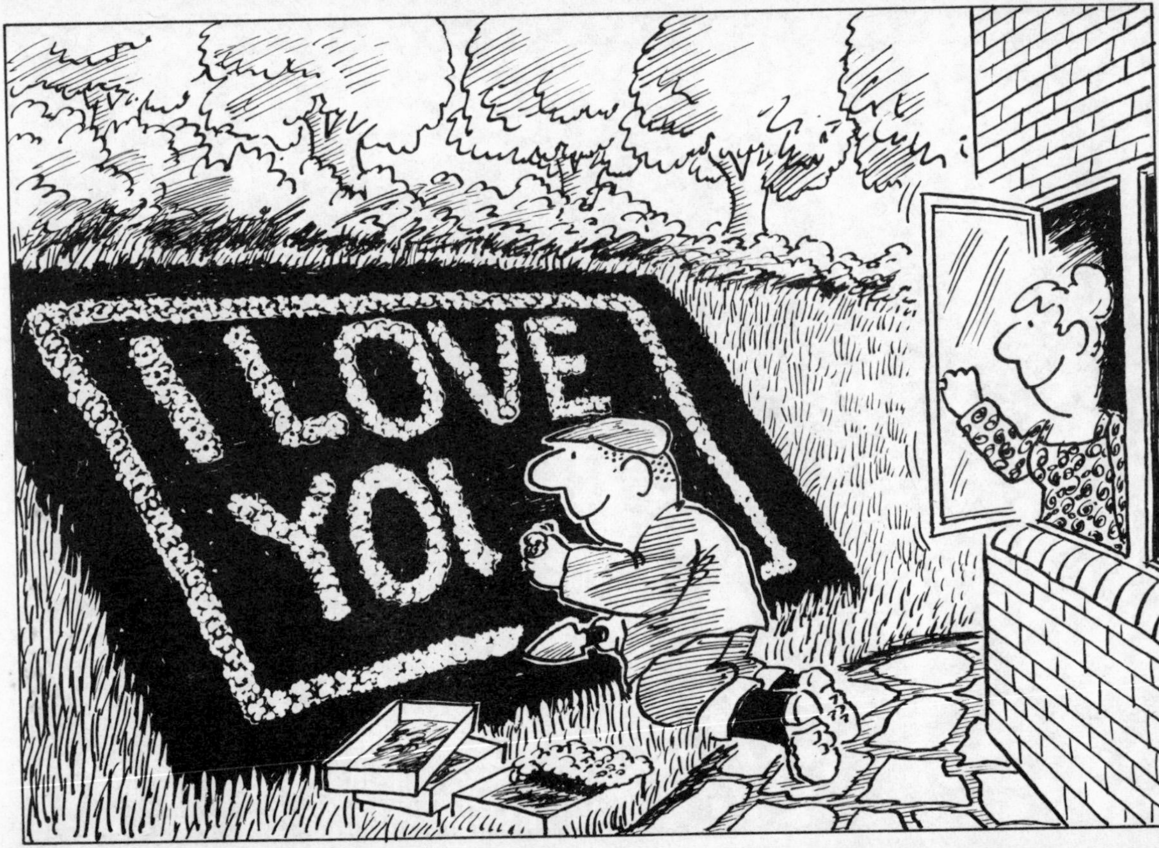
I LOVE
YO

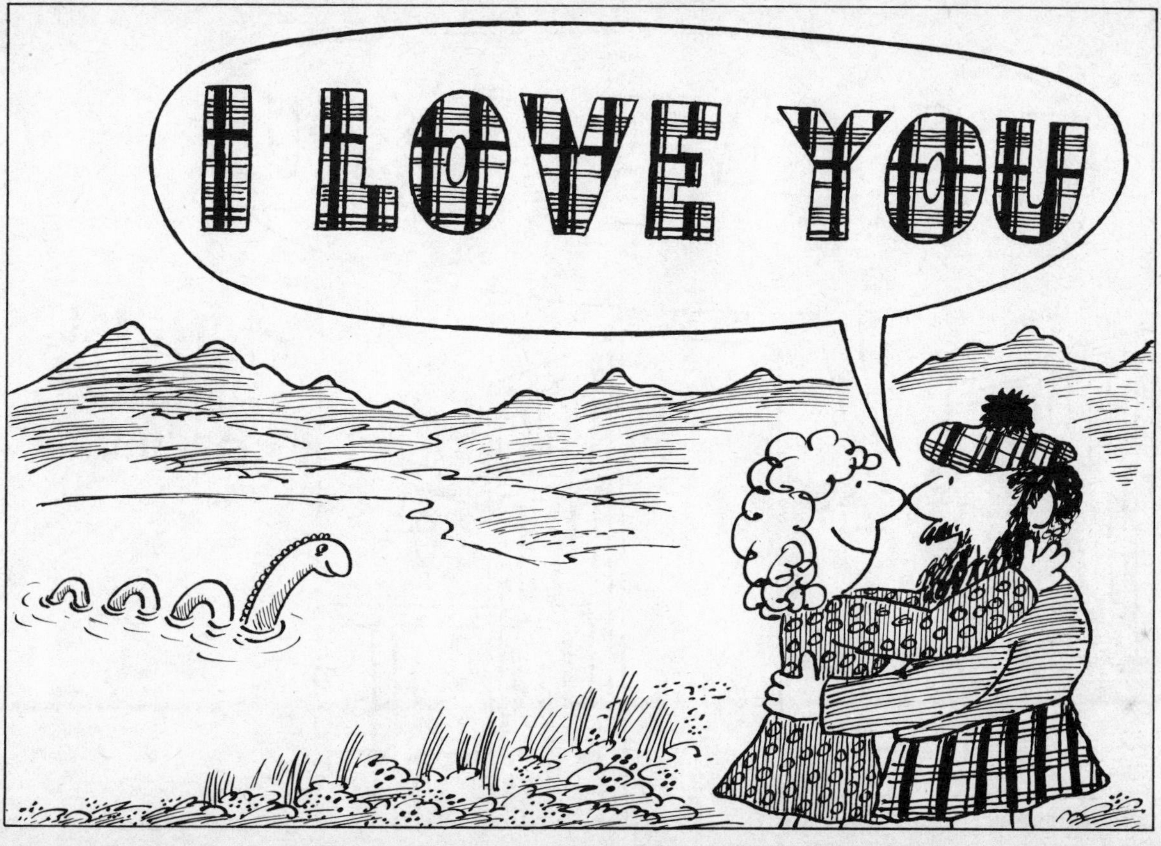
I LOVE YOU

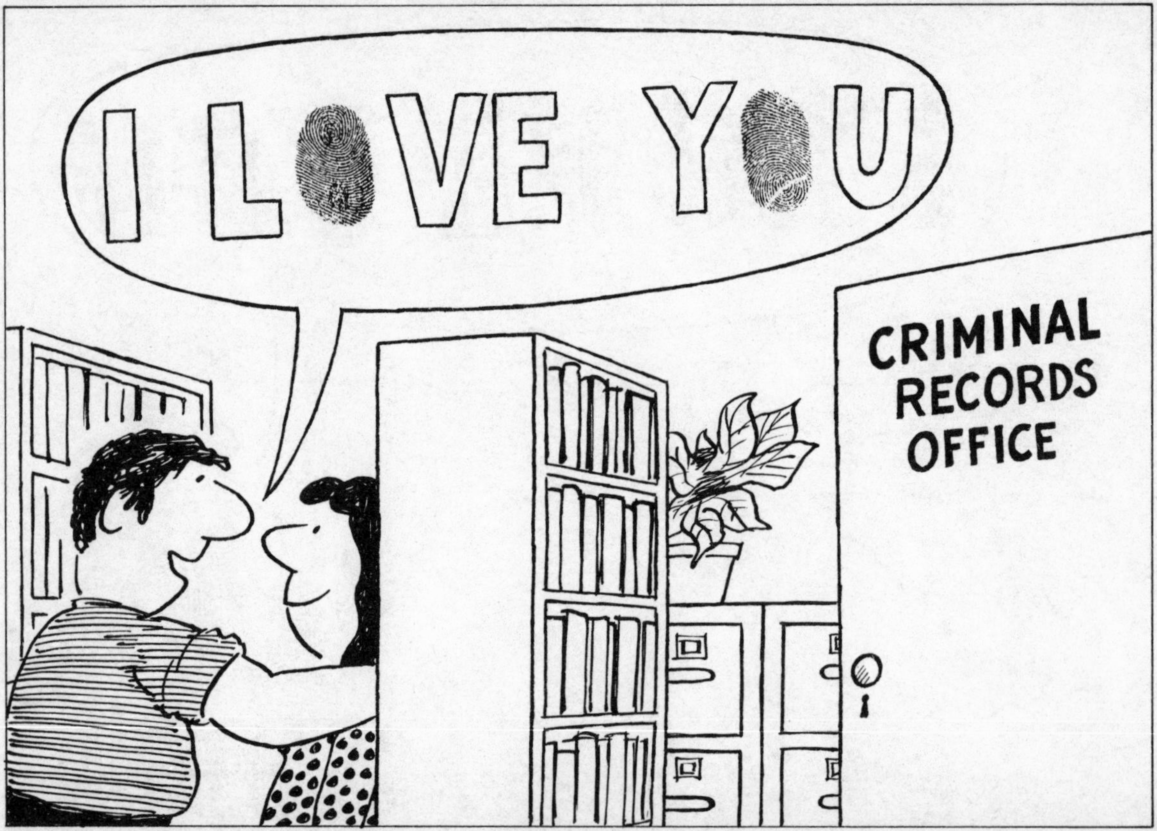
I LOVE YOU
CRIMINAL
RECORDS
OFFICE

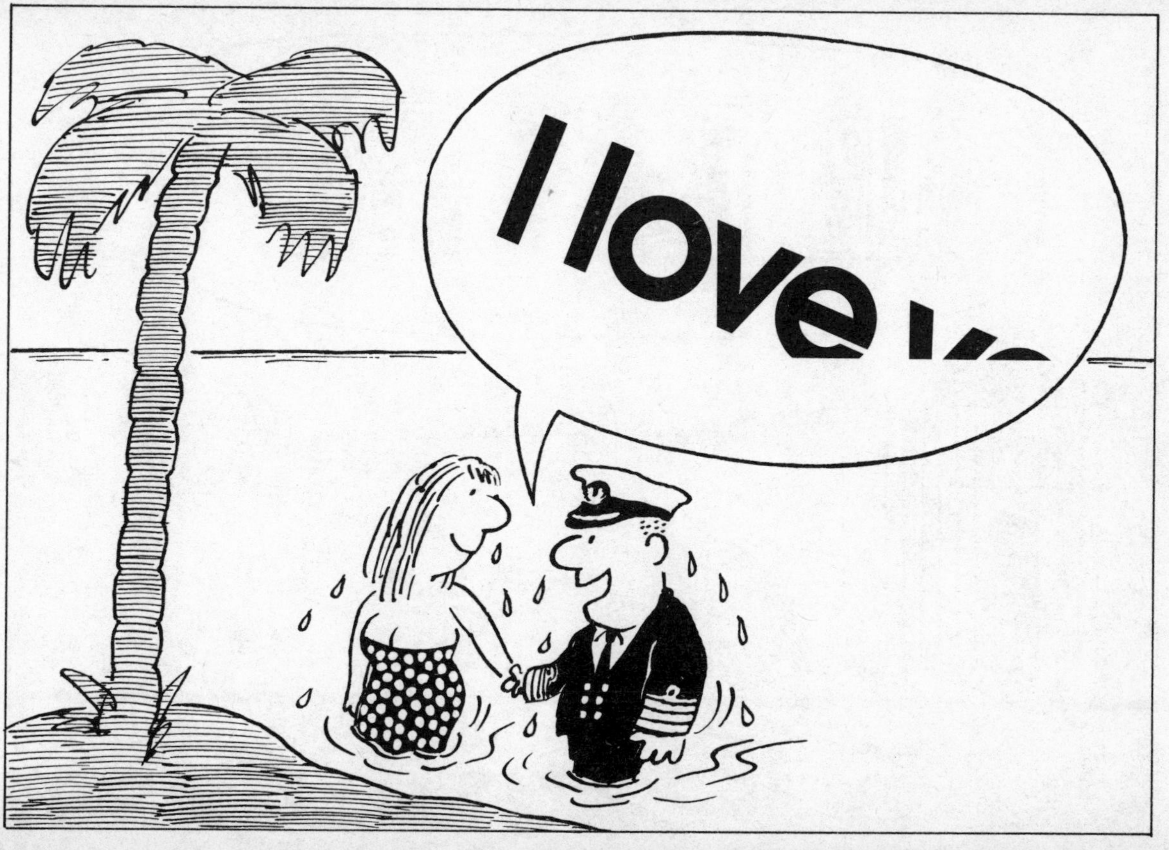
I love

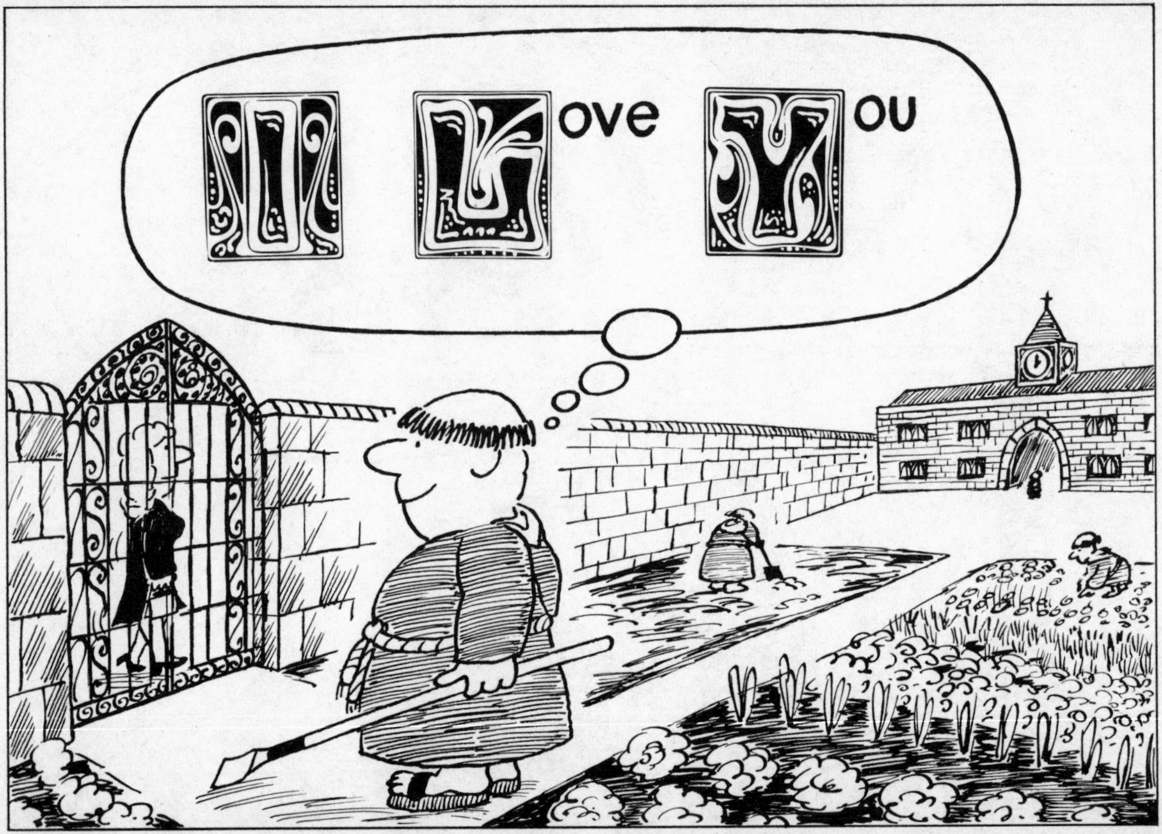
I Love You

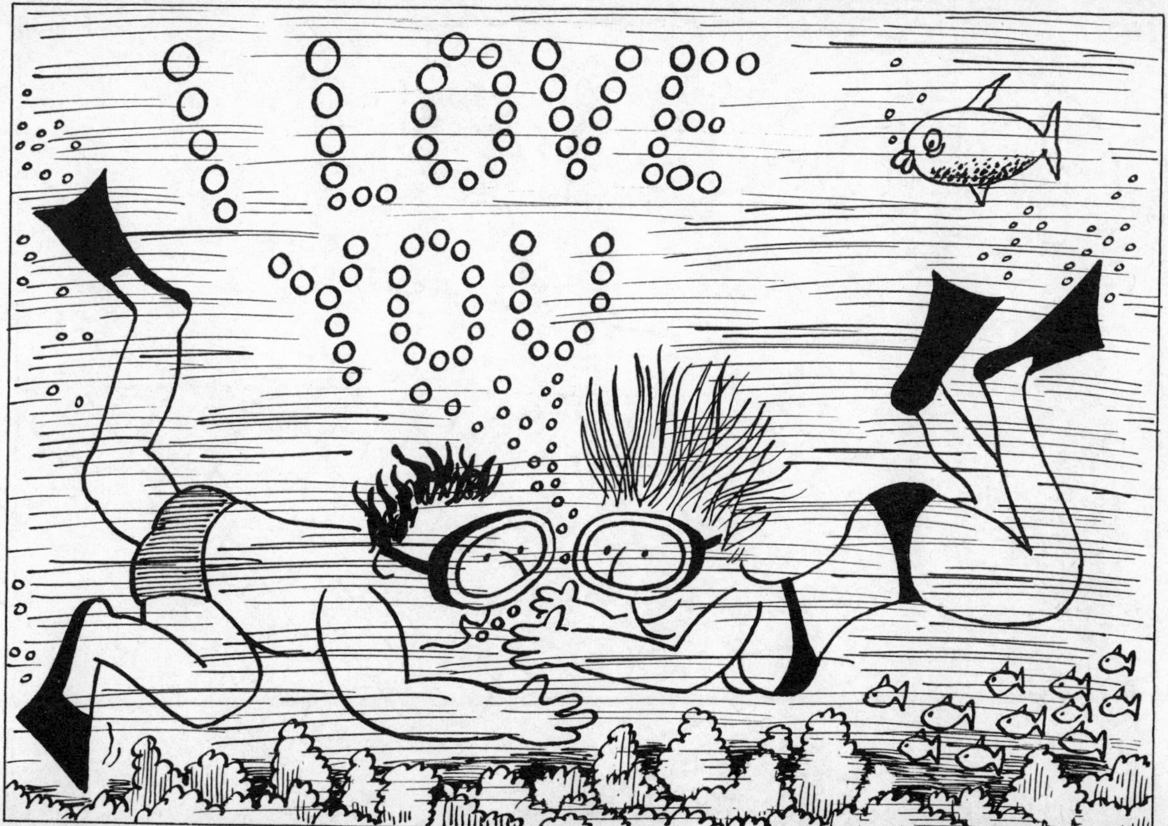
I LOVE YOU

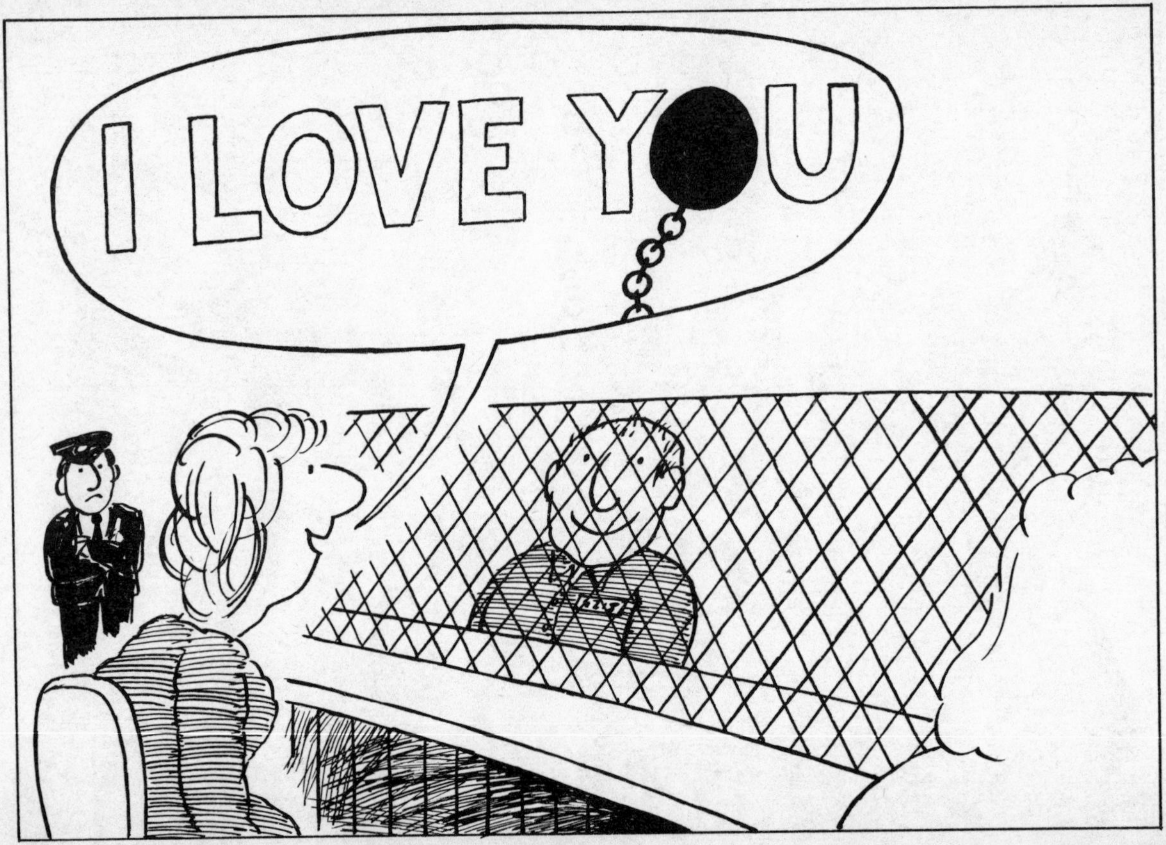
I LOVE YOU

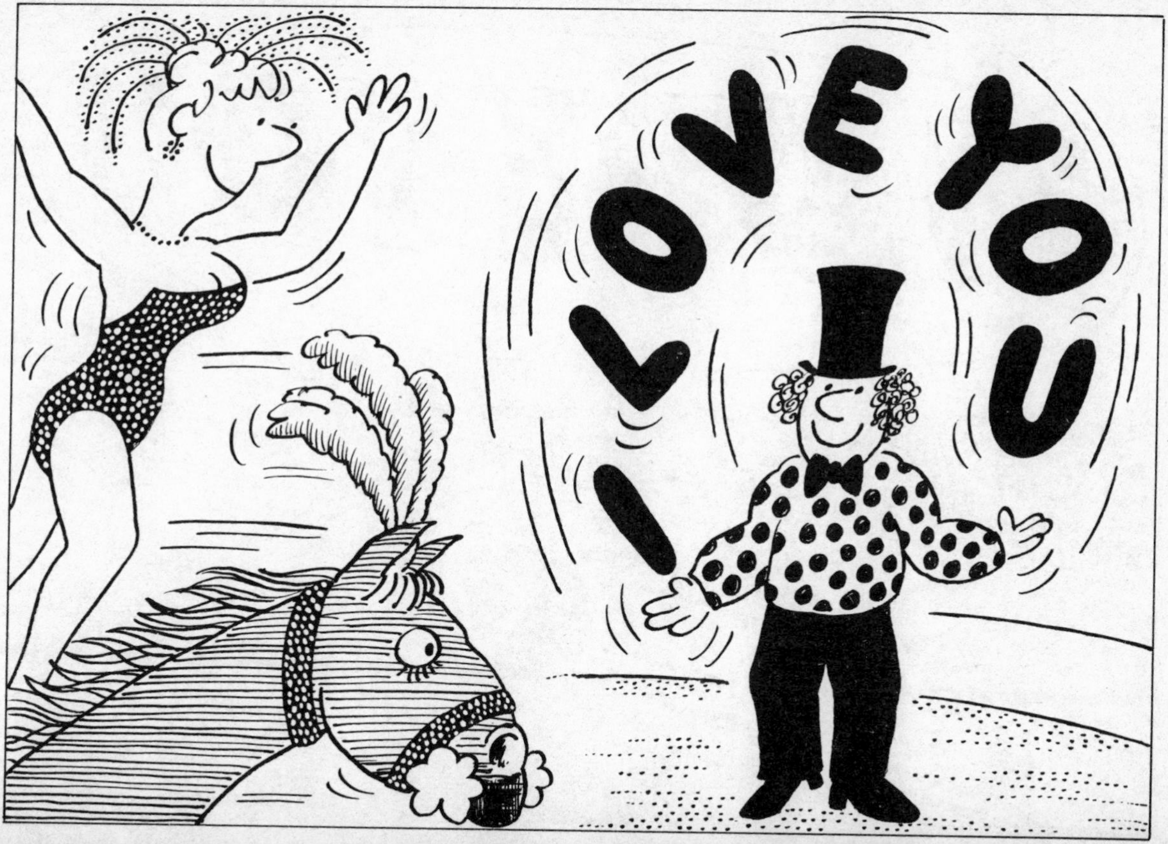
I LOVE YOU

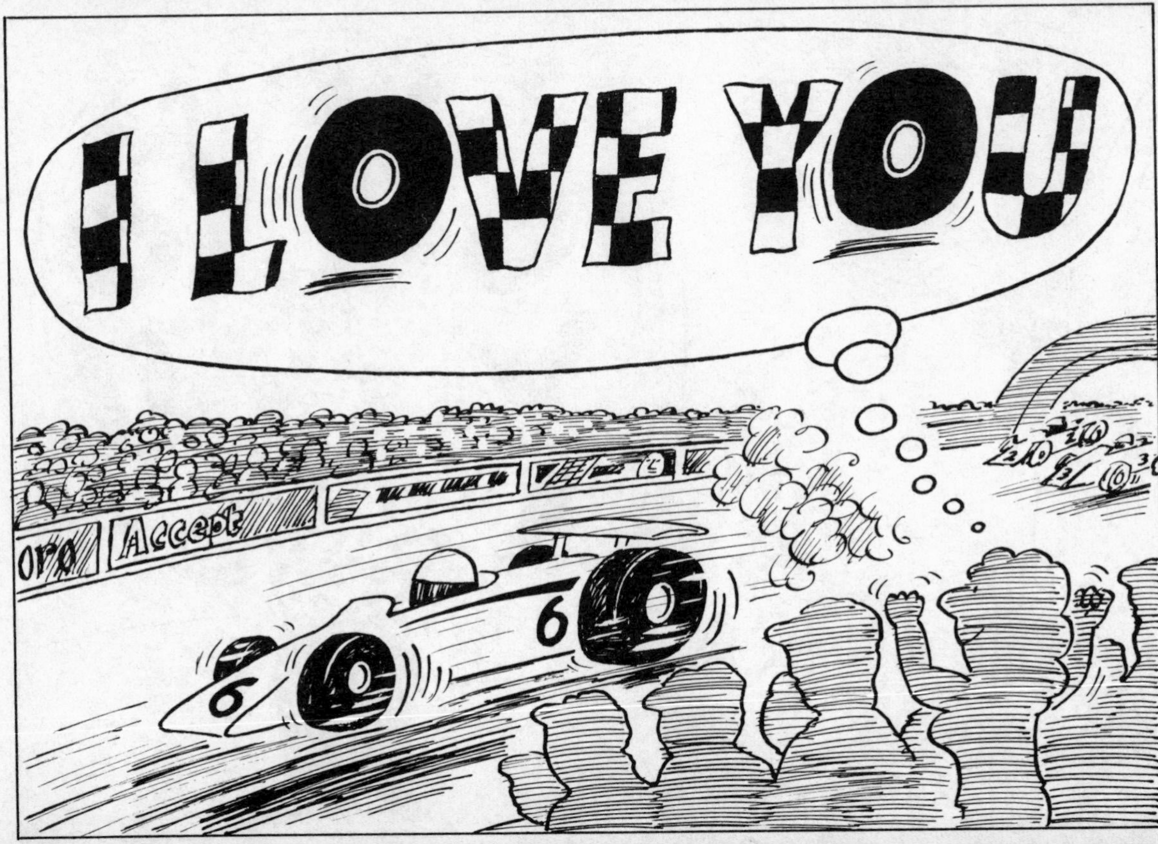
I LOVE YOU
Accept
oro

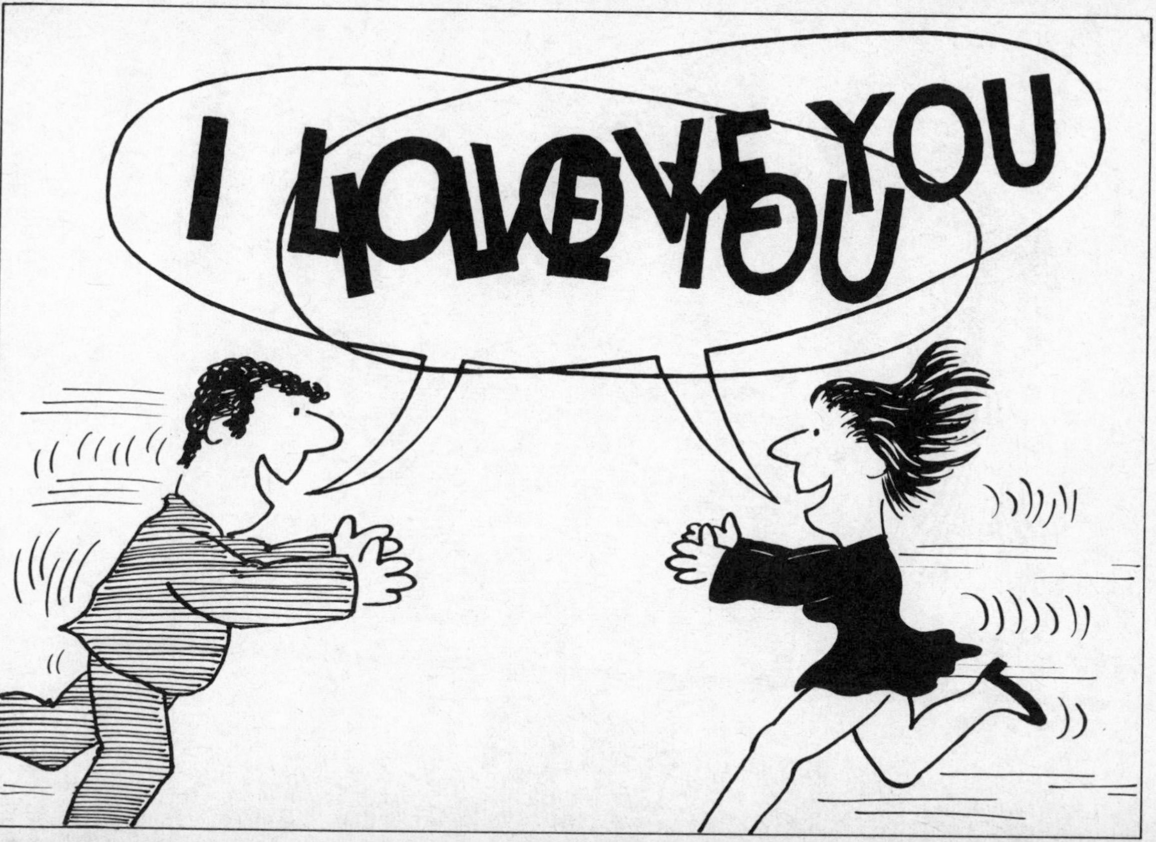
I LOVE YOU
I LOVE YOU

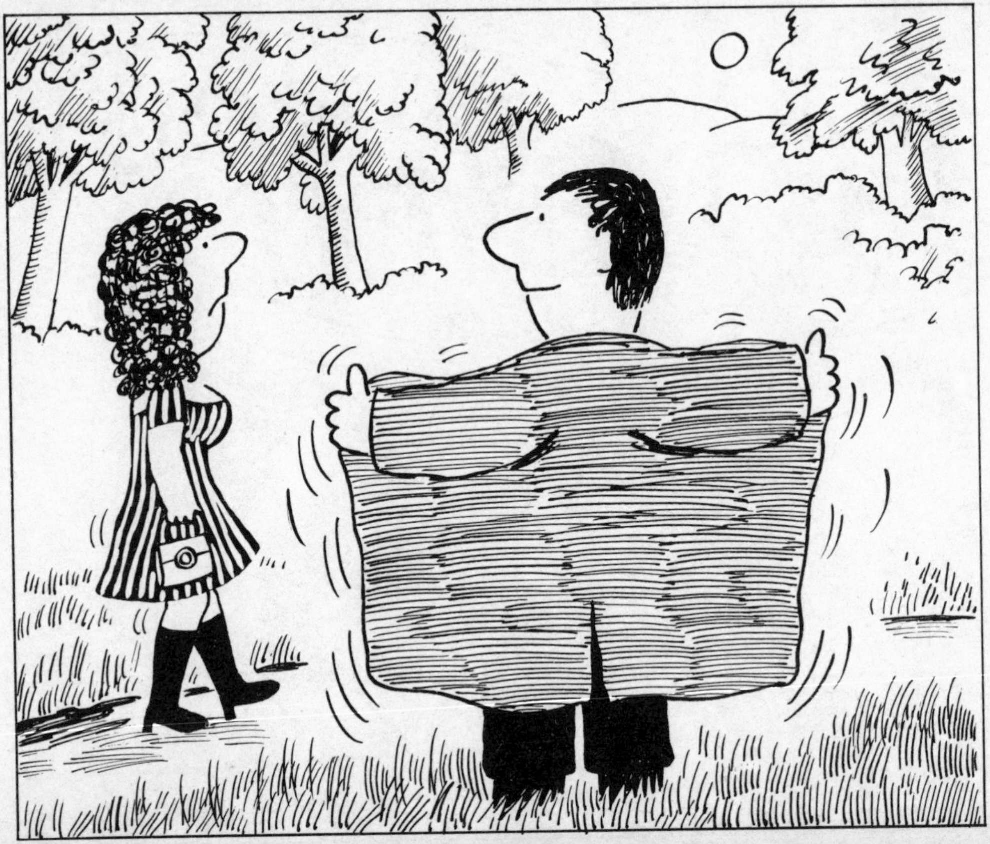

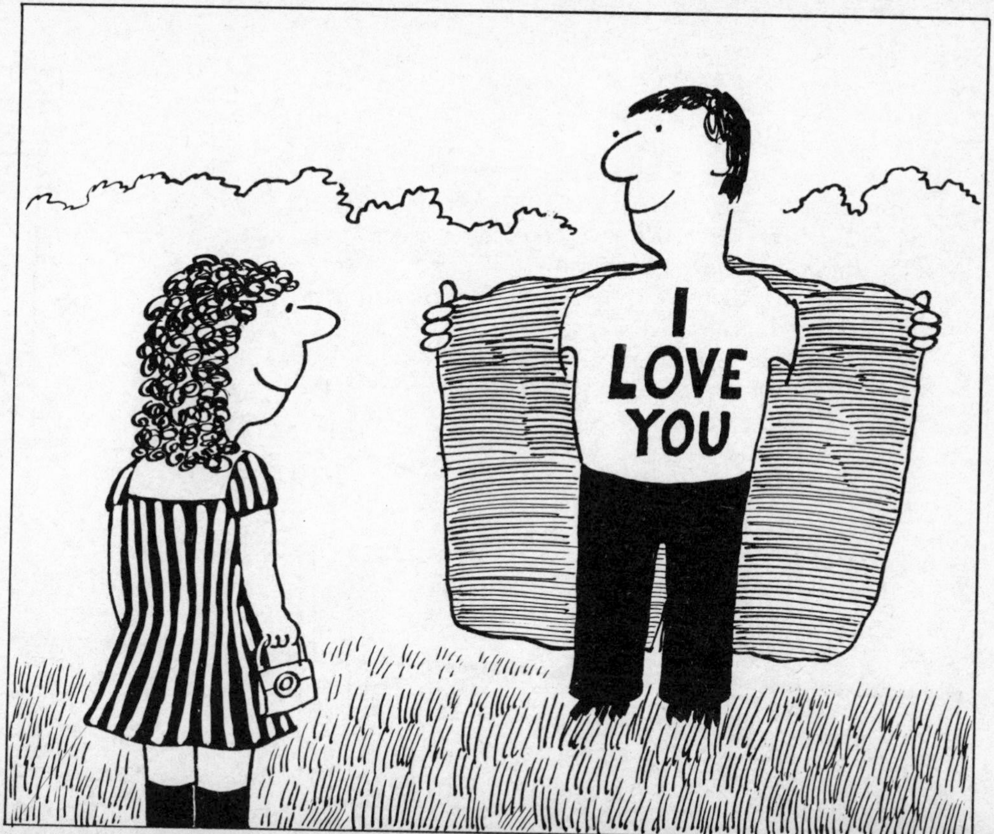
I
LOVE
YOU

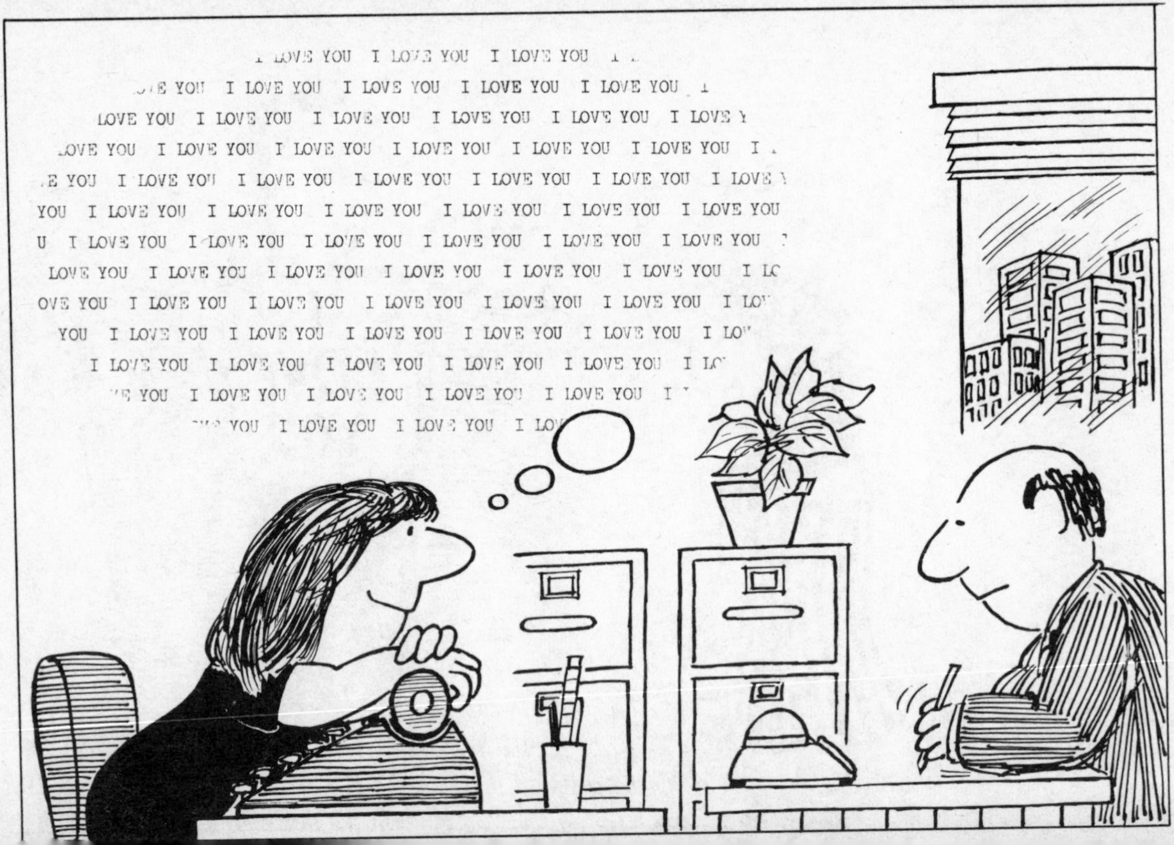
I LOVE YOU I LOVE YOU I LOVE YOU
YOU I LOVE YOU I LOVE YOU I LOVE YOU I LOVE YOU
LOVE YOU I LOVE YOU I LOVE YOU I LOVE YOU I LOVE YOU I LOVE
LOVE YOU I LOVE YOU I LOVE YOU I LOVE YOU I LOVE YOU I LOVE YOU I
YOU I LOVE YOU I LOVE YOU I LOVE YOU I LOVE YOU I LOVE YOU I LOVE
YOU I LOVE YOU I LOVE YOU I LOVE YOU I LOVE YOU I LOVE YOU I LOVE YOU
U I LOVE YOU I LOVE YOU I LOVE YOU I LOVE YOU I LOVE YOU I LOVE YOU
LOVE YOU I LOVE YOU I LOVE YOU I LOVE YOU I LOVE YOU I LOVE YOU
OVE YOU I LOVE YOU I LOVE YOU I LOVE YOU I LOVE YOU I LOVE YOU
YOU I LOVE YOU I LOVE YOU I LOVE YOU I LOVE YOU I LOVE YOU
I LOVE YOU I LOVE YOU I LOVE YOU I LOVE YOU I LOVE YOU
YOU I LOVE YOU I LOVE YOU I LOVE YOU I LOVE YOU I
YOU I LOVE YOU I LOVE YOU

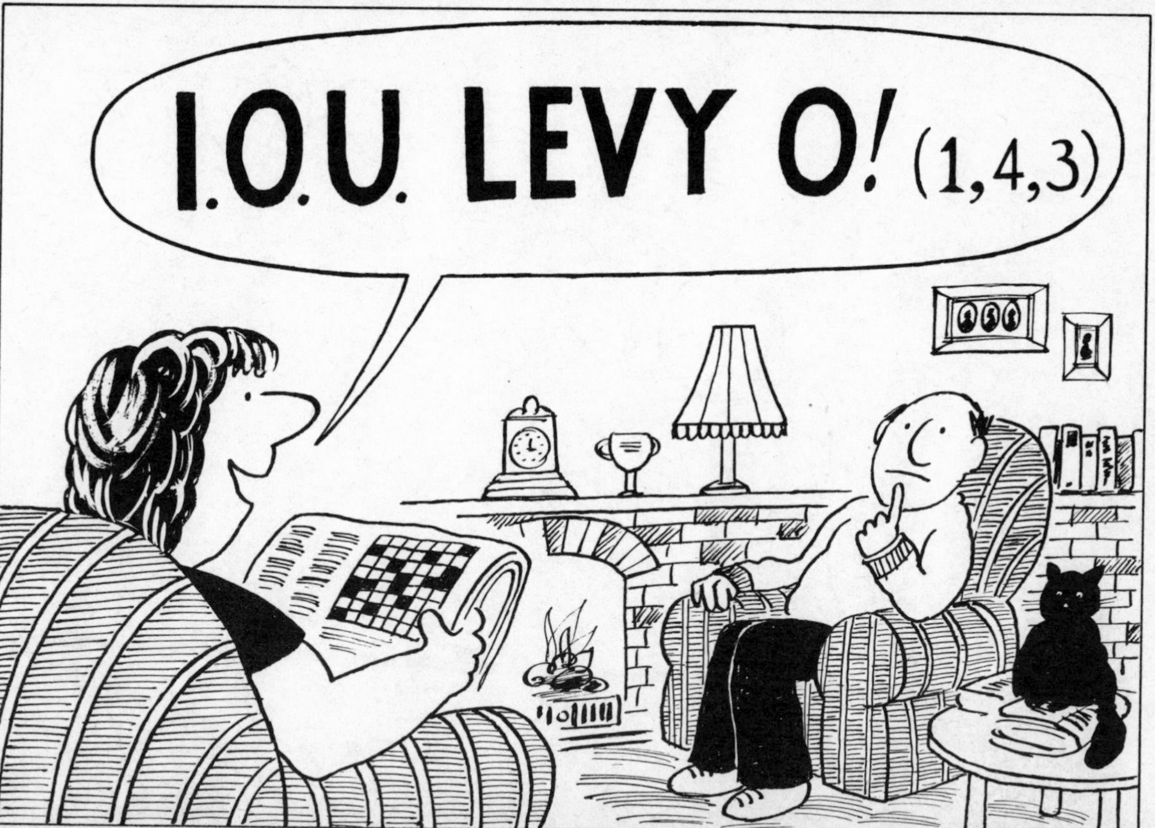
I.O.U. LEVY O! (1,4,3)

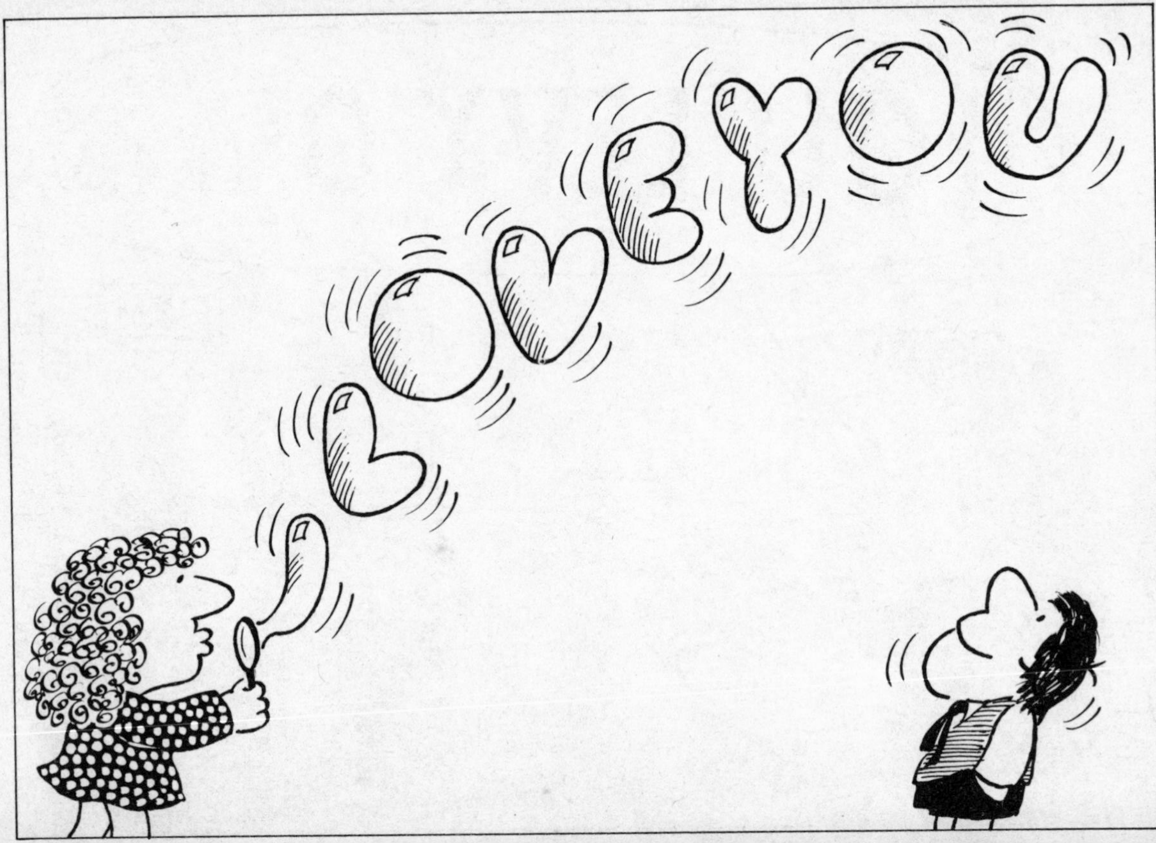
I LOVE YOU

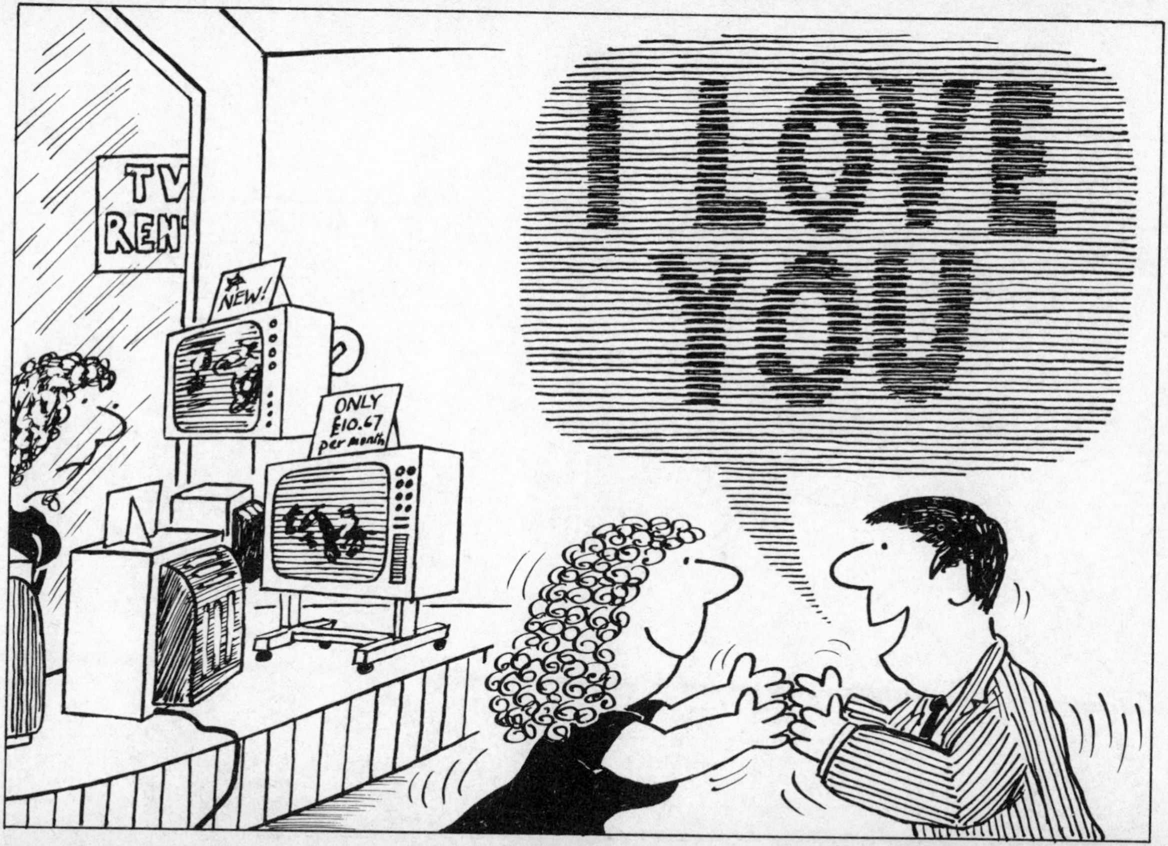
I LOVE YOU
TV REN
NEW!
ONLY £10.67 per month

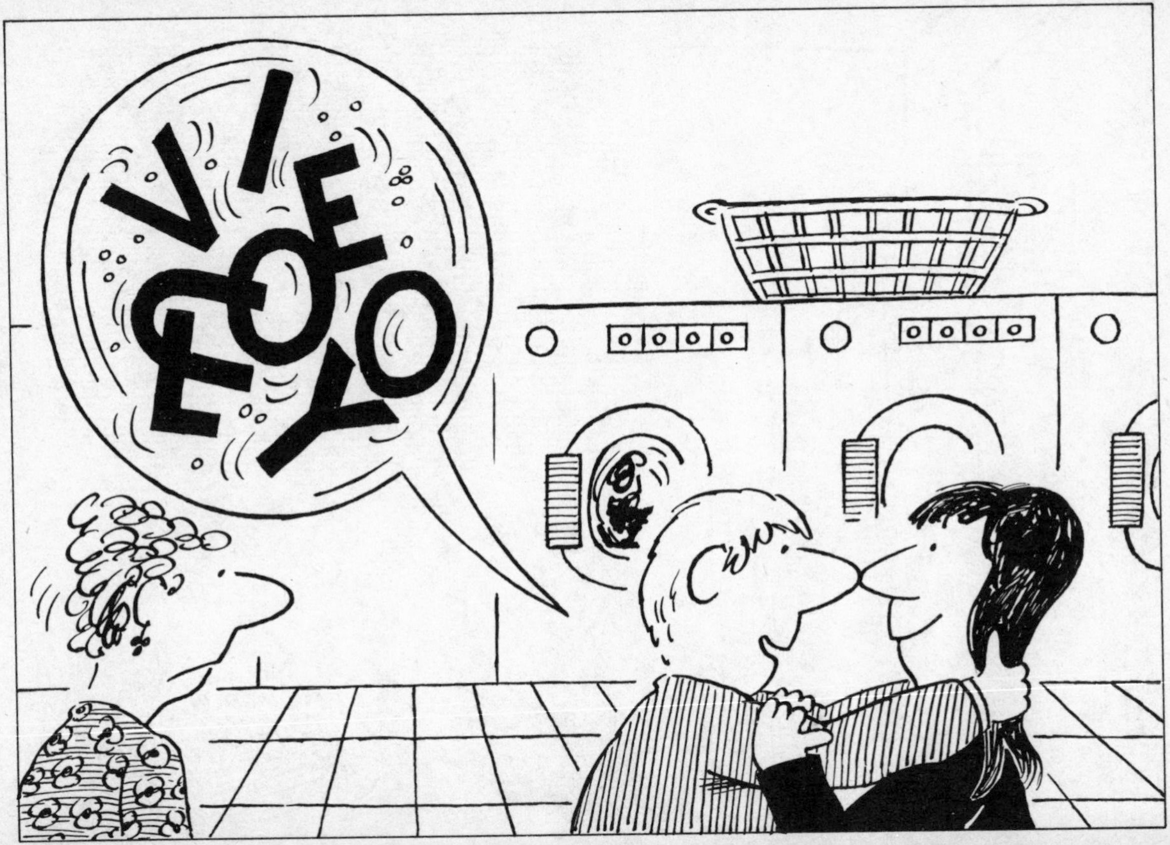

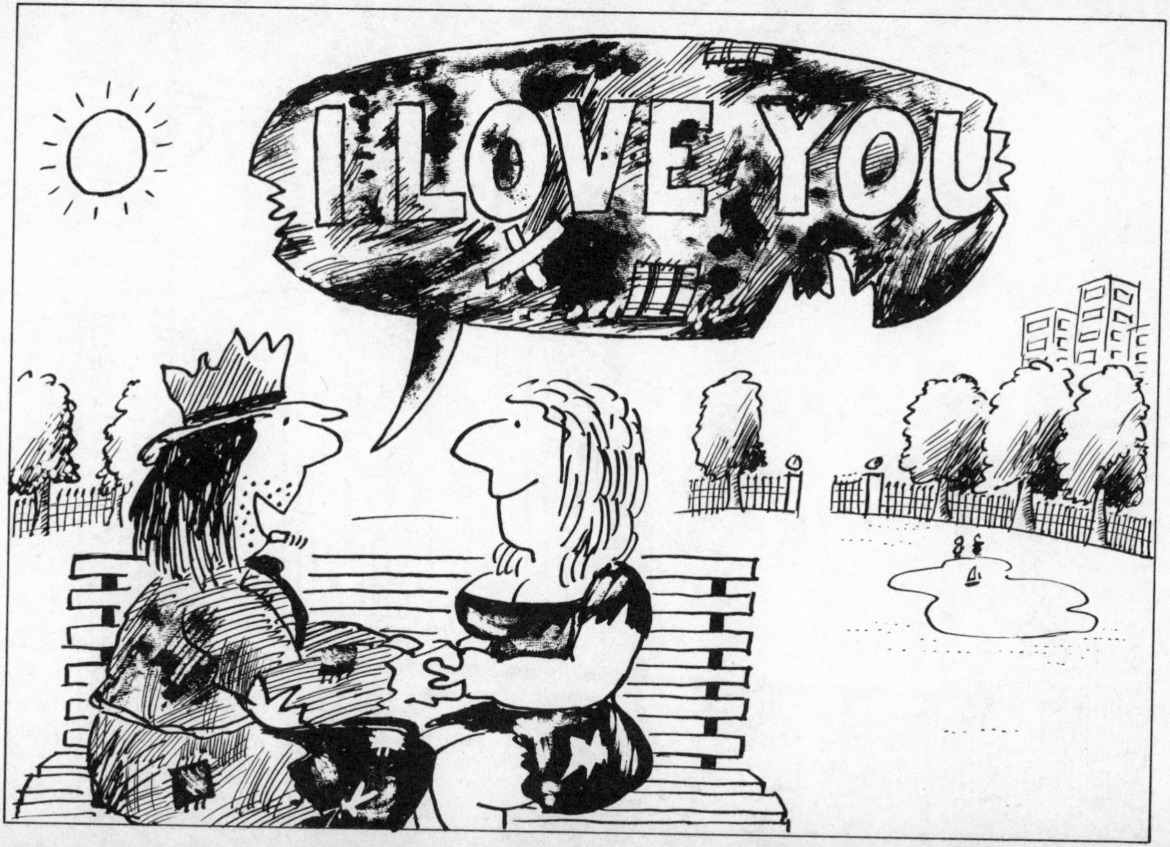
I LOVE YOU

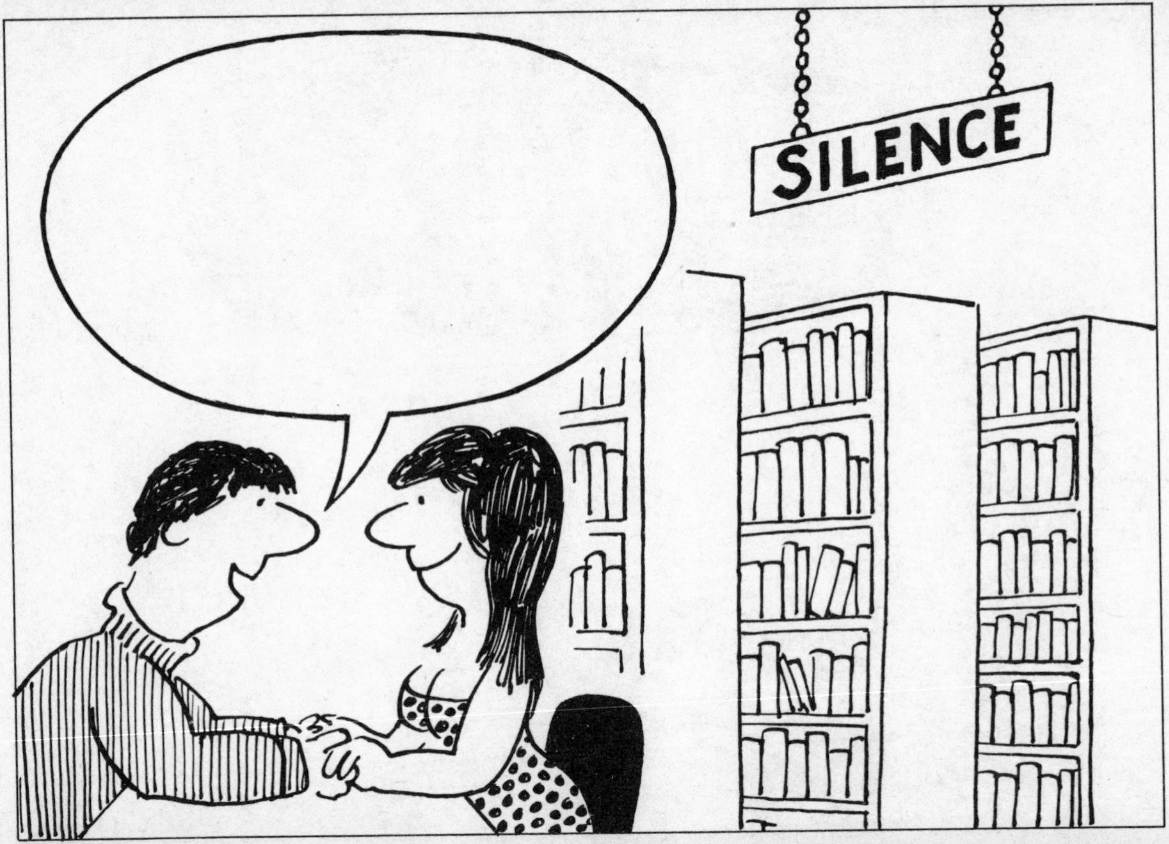
SILENCE

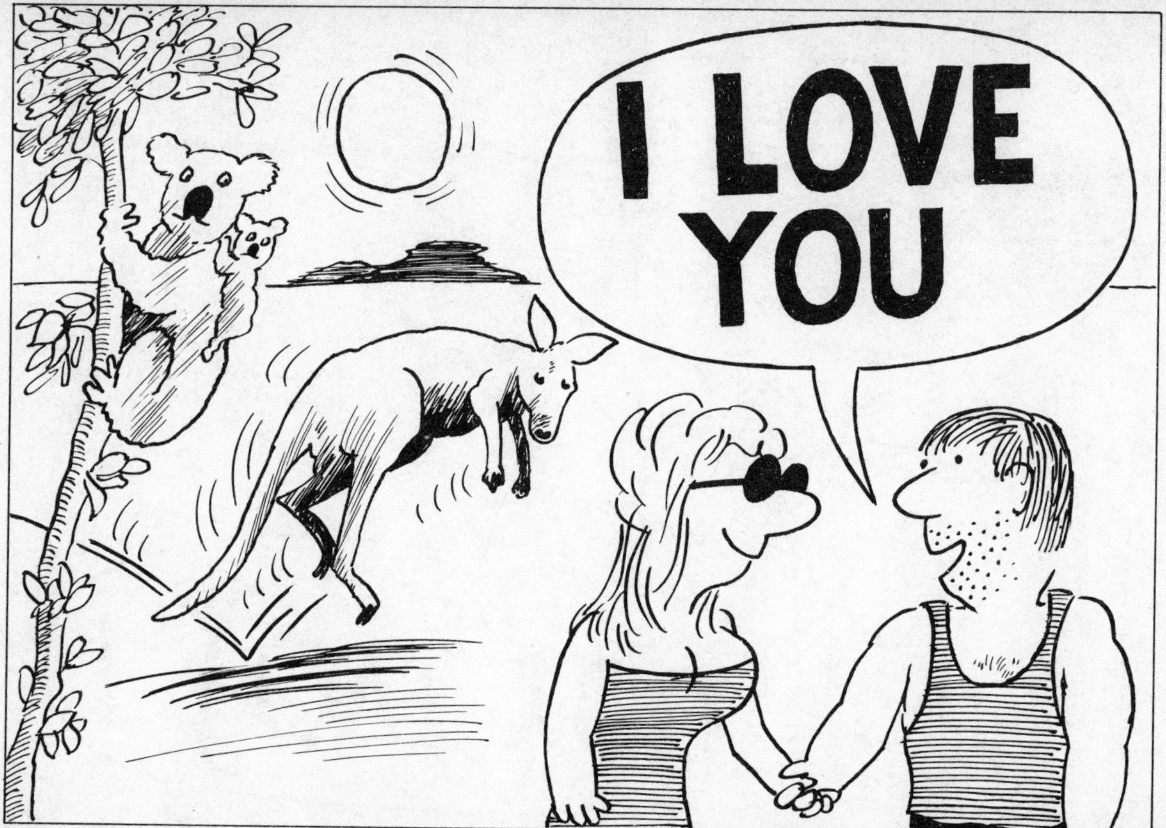
I LOVE YOU

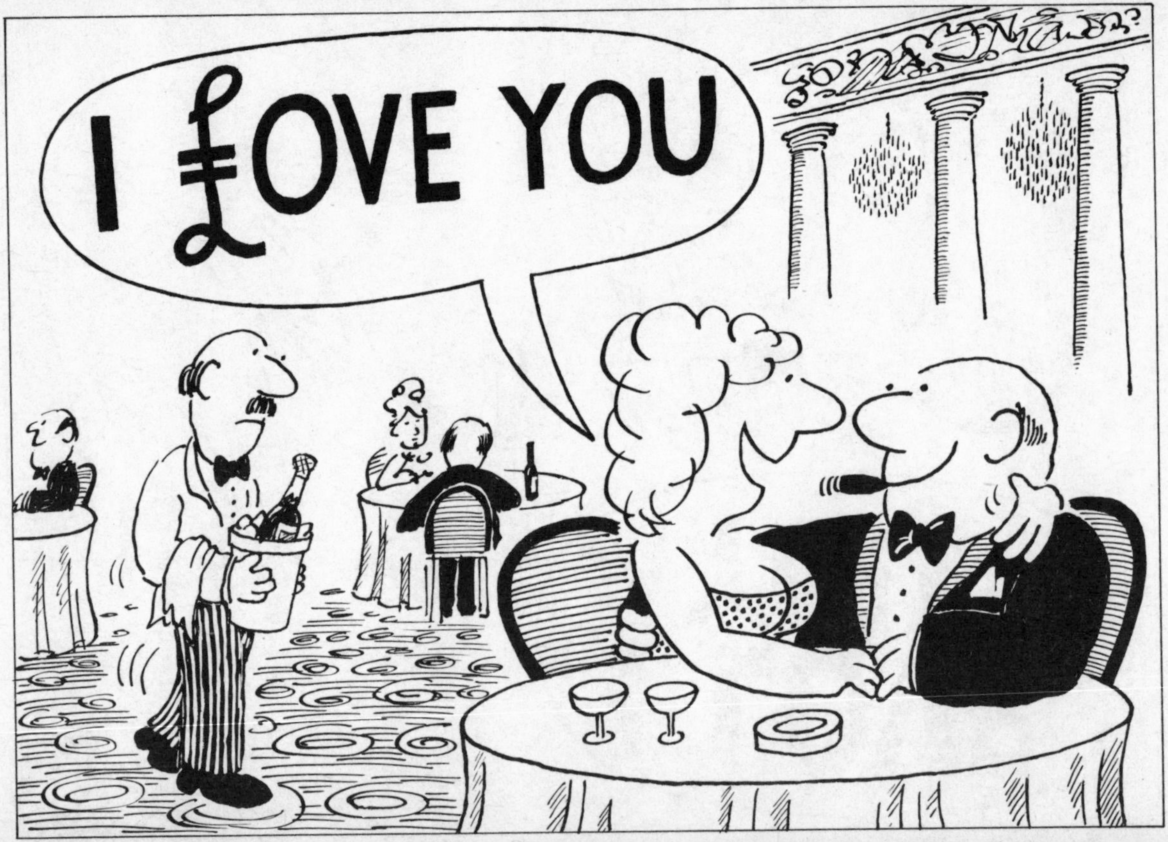
I £OVE YOU

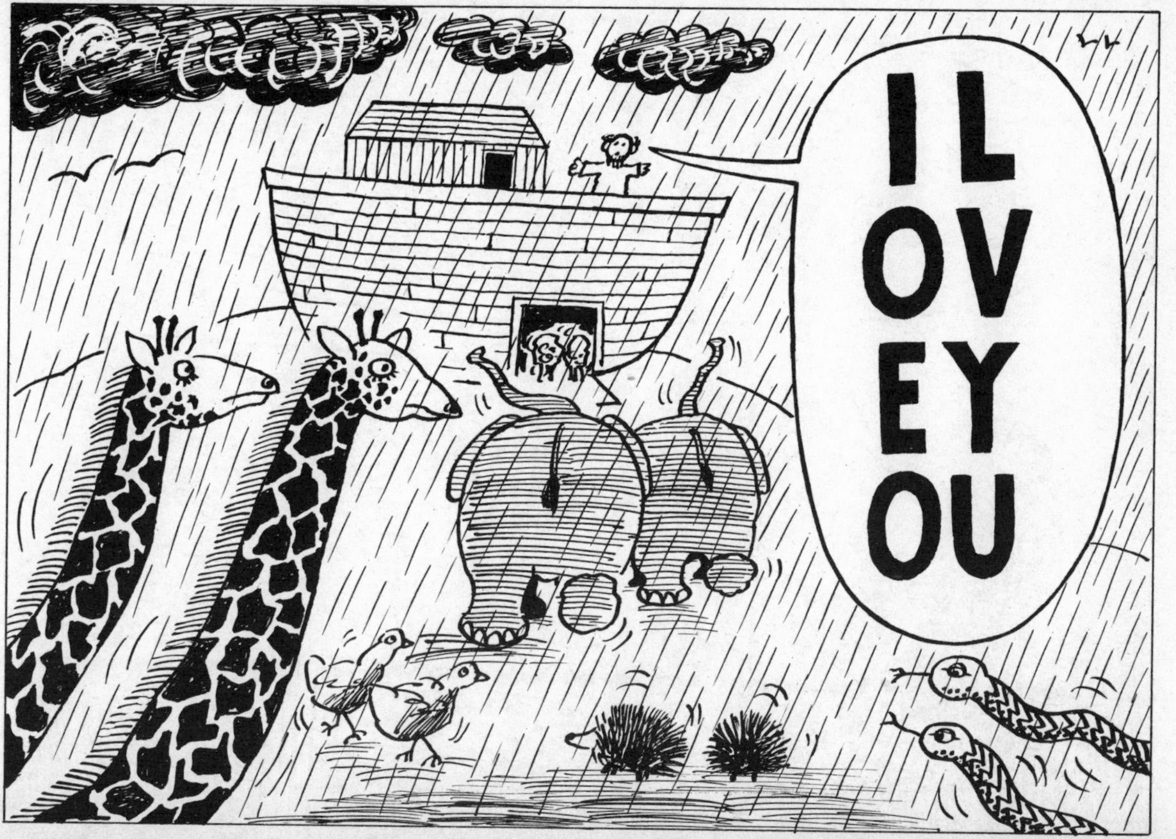
I L
O V
E Y
O U

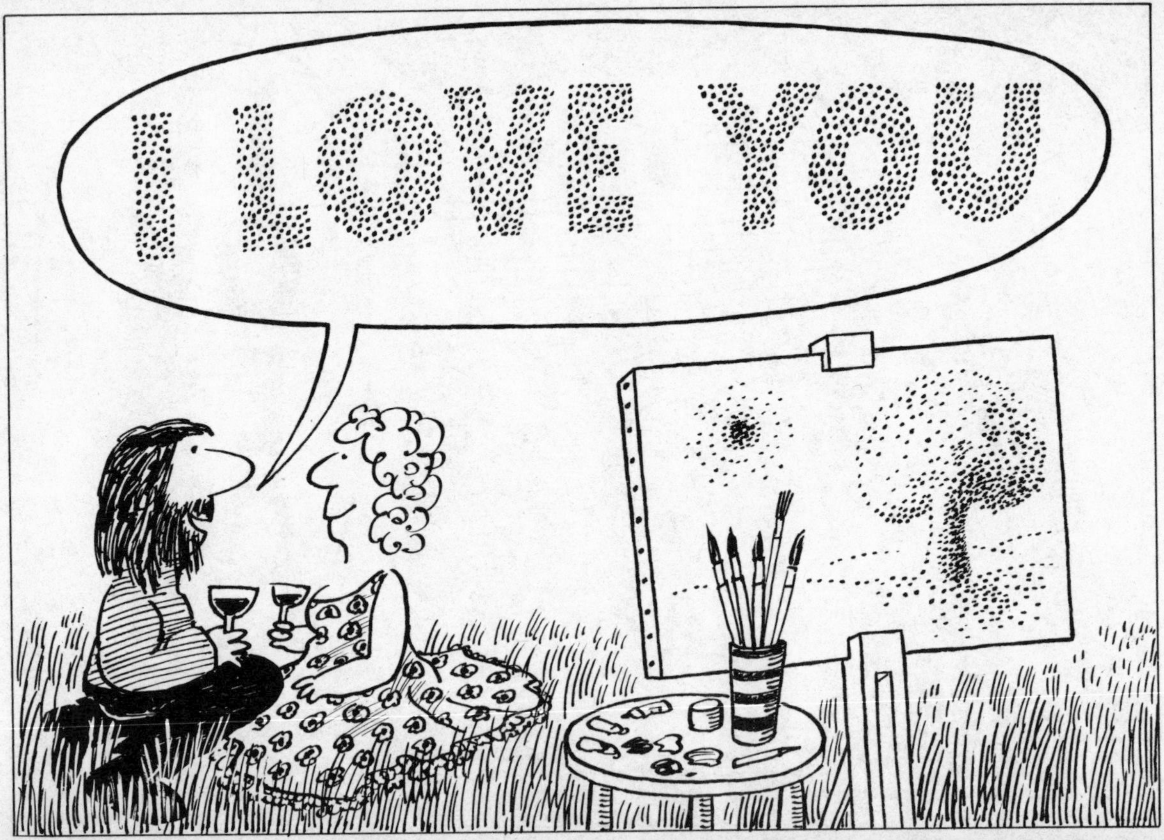
I LOVE YOU

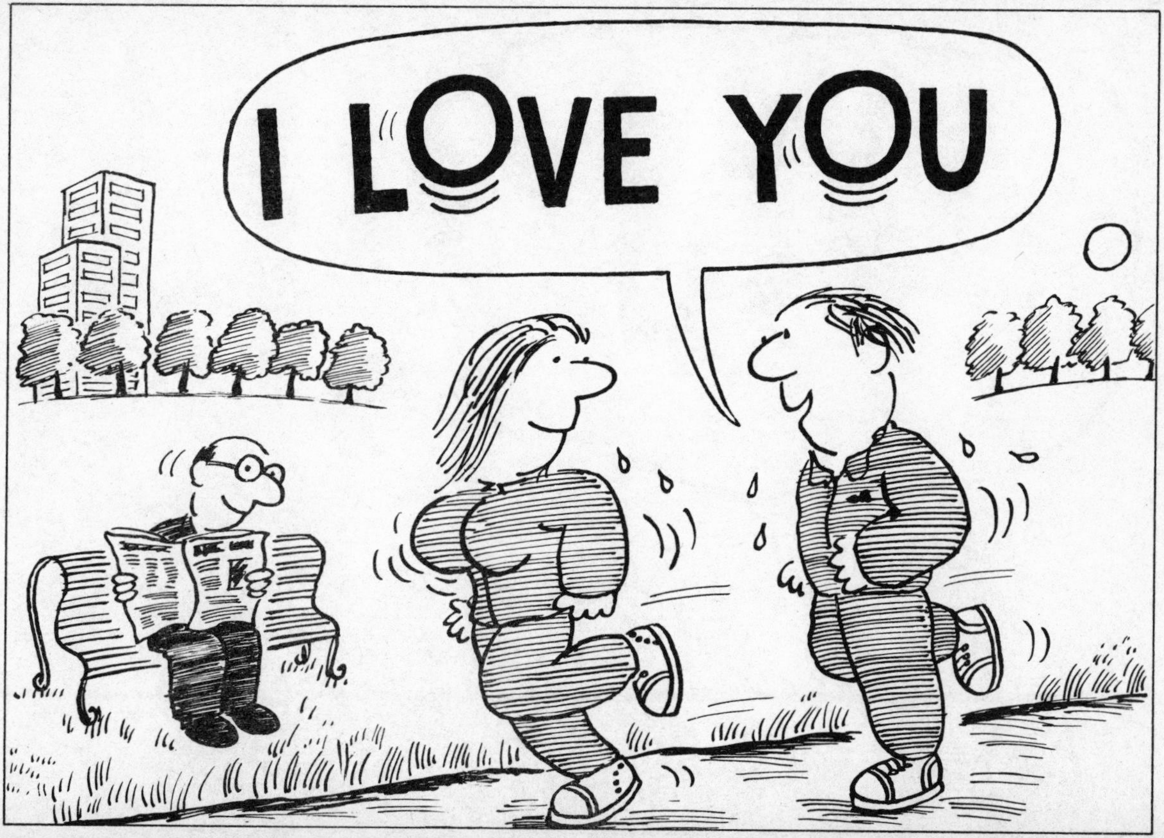
I LOVE YOU

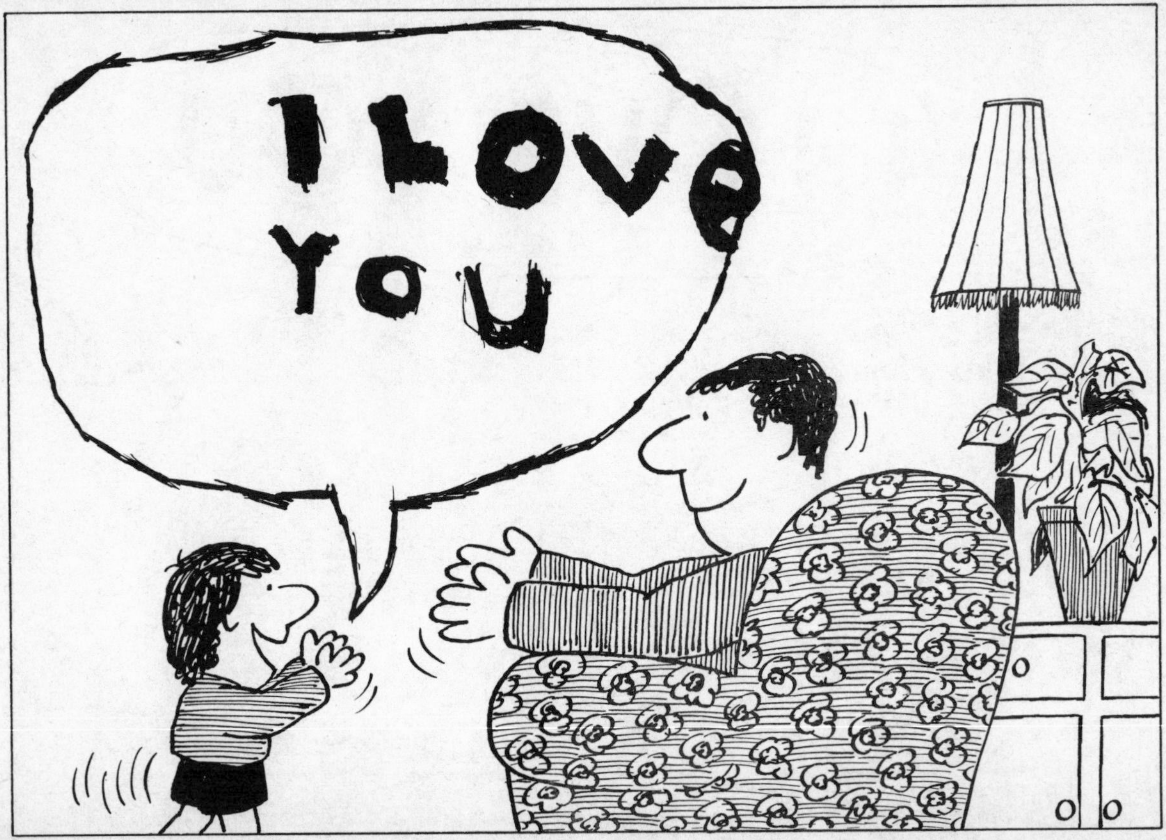
I LOVE YOU

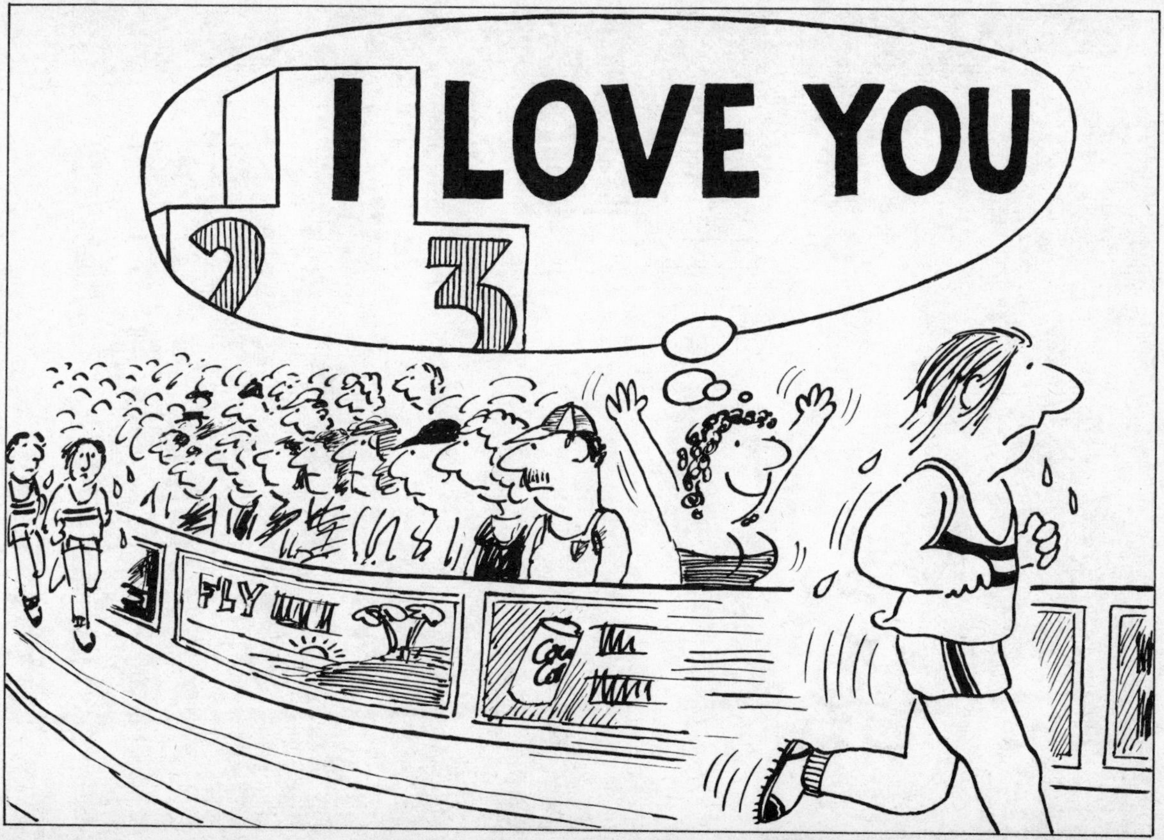

I LOVE YOU
2
3
FLY

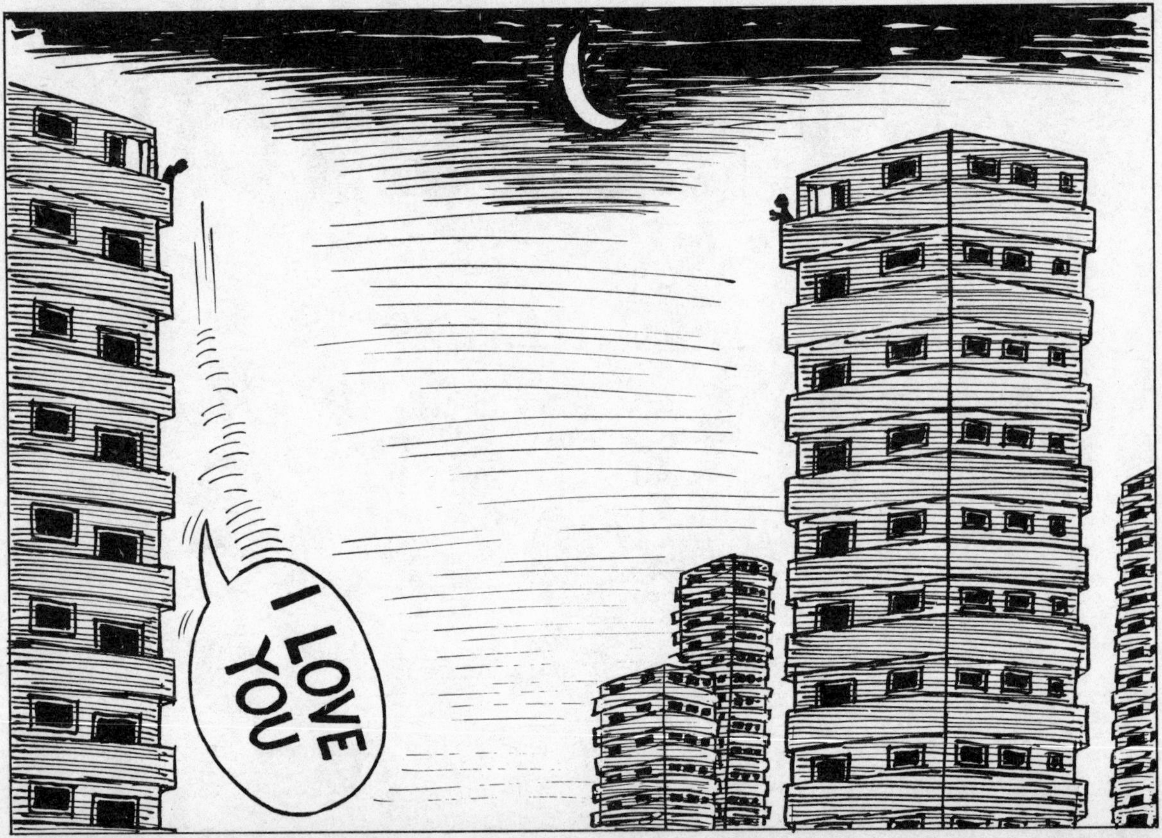
I LOVE YOU

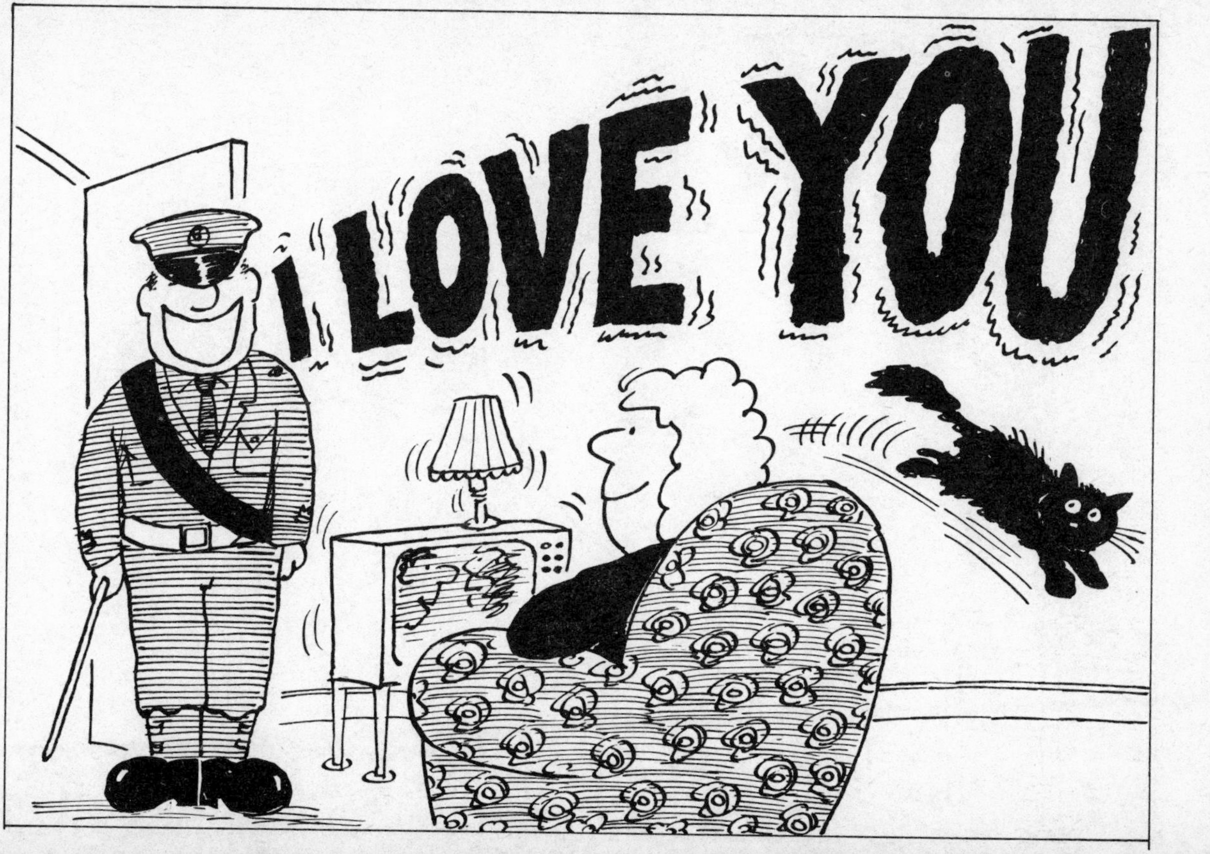
I LOVE YOU

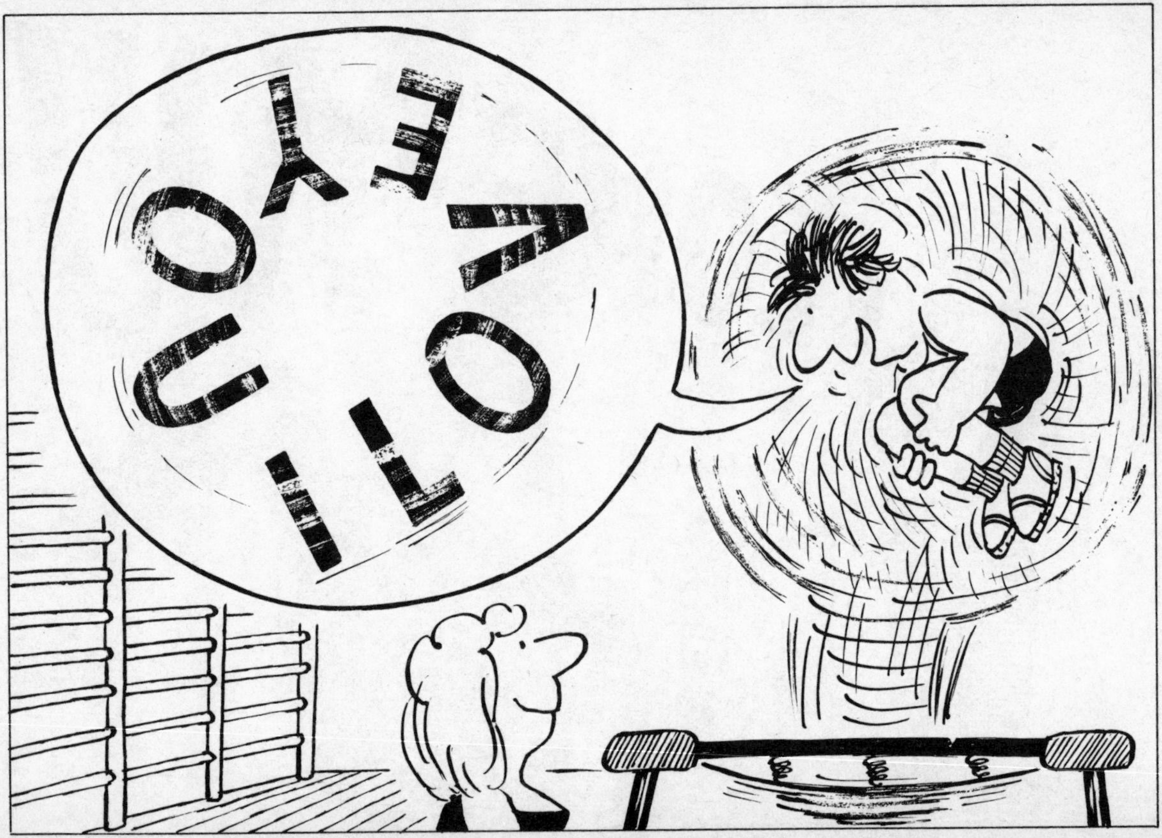
I LOVE YOU

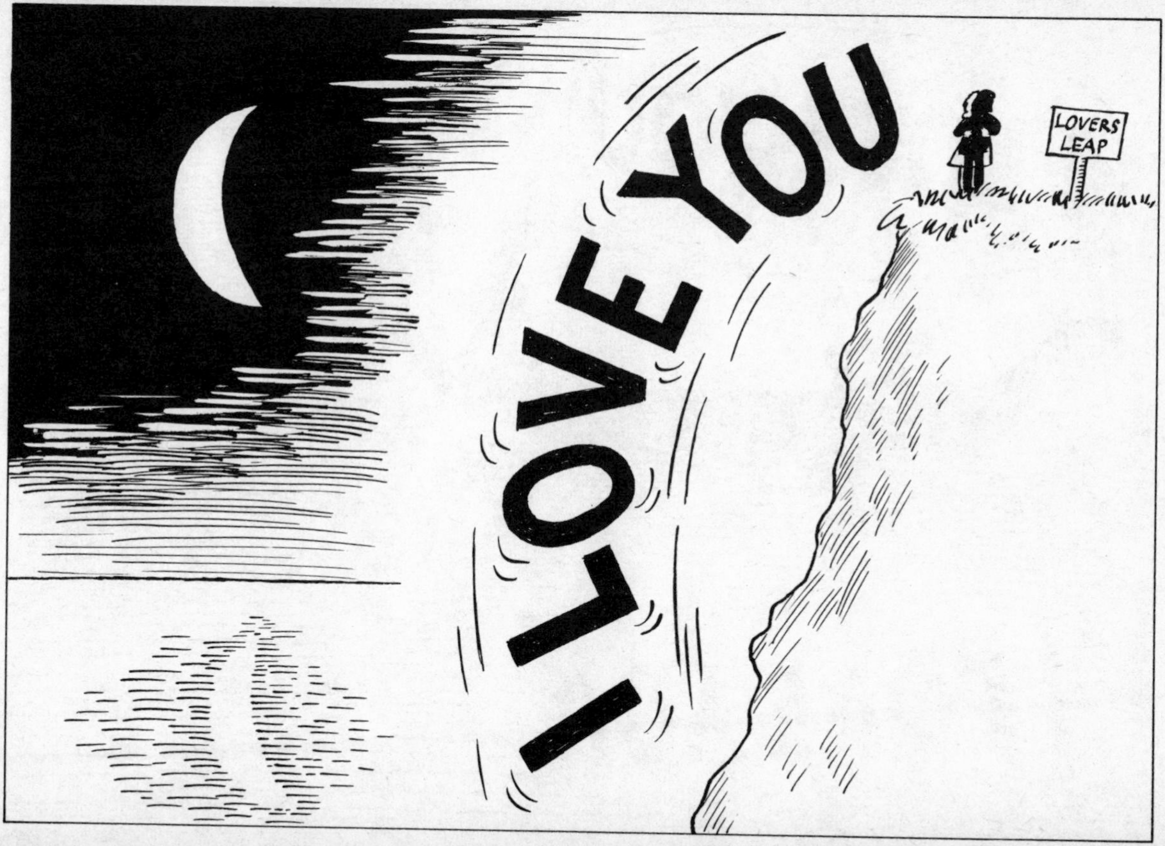
I LOVE YOU
LOVERS LEAP

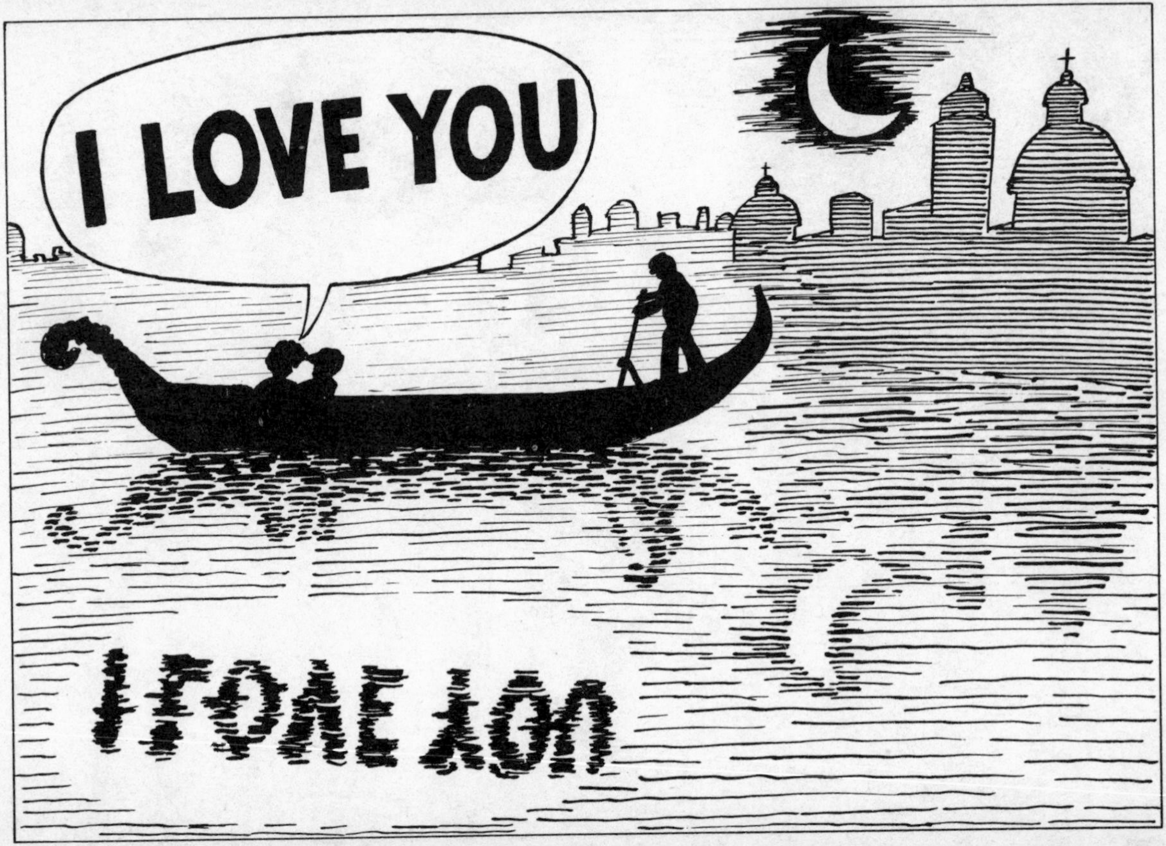
I LOVE YOU

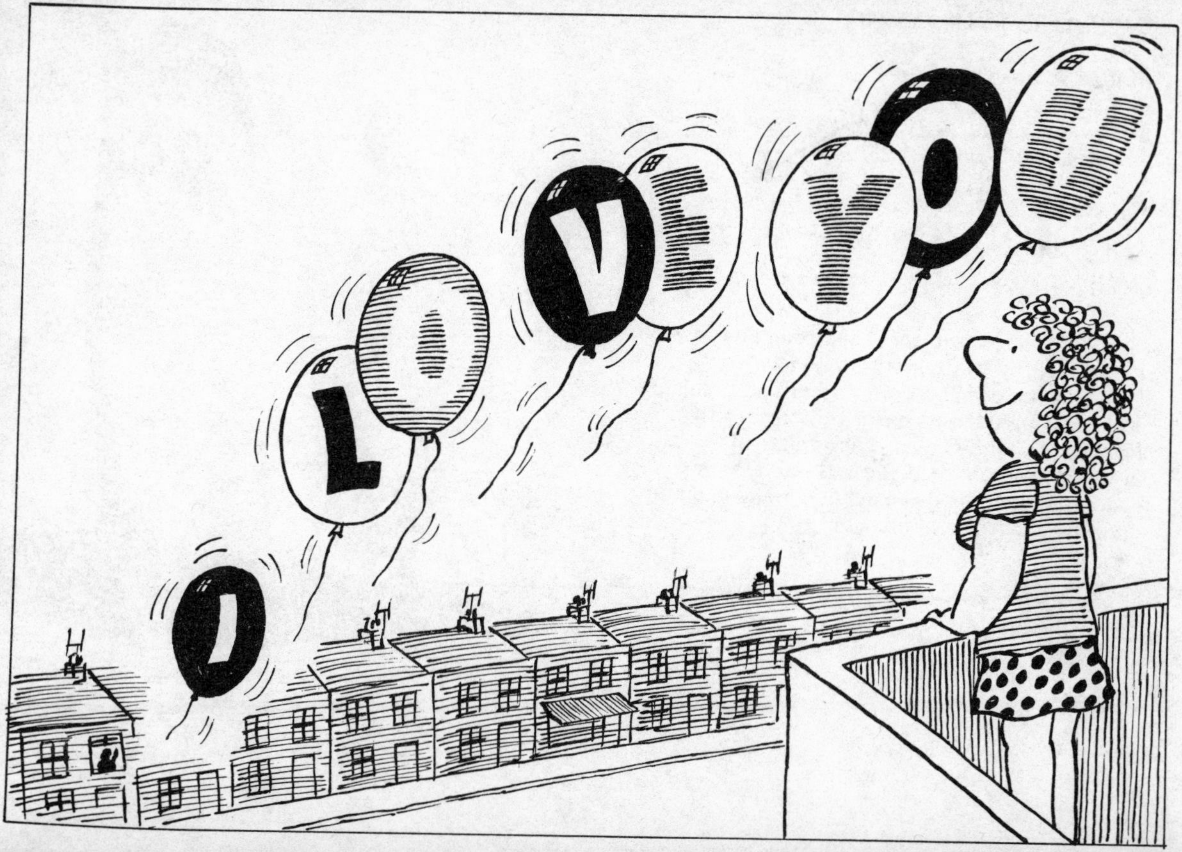
I LOVE YOU

Printed and bound in Great Britain by
Pitman Press Ltd, Bath
for the Publishers, W.H. Allen & Co. Ltd,
44 Hill Street, London WIX 8LB

ISBN 0 491 03002 9 (W.H. Allen hardcover edition)
0 352 31389 7 (Star Books softcover edition)

Reprinted 1984

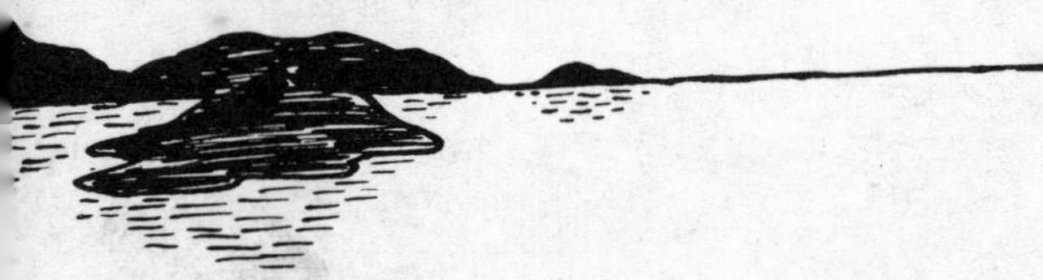
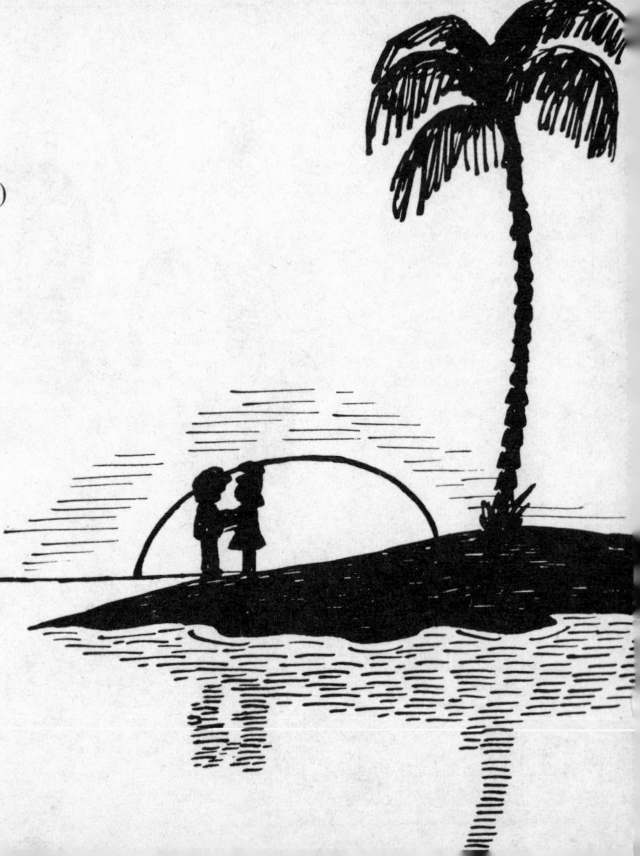